ALSO BY JOSHUA S. PORTER

Punk Rock vs the Lizard People

Death to Deconstruction: Reclaiming Faithfulness as an Act of Rebellion

WITH ALL ITS TEETH

WITH ALL ITS TEETH

SEX, VIOLENCE, PROFANITY, AND THE DEATH OF CHRISTIAN ART

Joshua S. Porter

For Isla.
If you want to sing,
sing.

CONTENTS

"The definition of Christian art is to be found in its subject and its spirit. Everything, sacred and profane, belongs to it. God does not ask for 'religious' art or 'Catholic' art. The art he wants for himself is Art, with all its teeth."

JACQUES MARITAIN

"Art is not a crime… Unless you do it right."

ARREX, PORTLAND STREET ARTIST

PROLOGUE
WHAT HELL SMELLS LIKE

THE PAPER MILL IN Savannah, Georgia, smelled like rot. "It's what hell smells like," my mom told me, craning her neck toward the backseat of the car. "Fire and brimstone," she said, scrunching her nose to indicate stench. My dad worked there for decades, company coveralls, a hardhat, the whole thing. Some weekends, we'd meet him there, at the paper mill, before a family outing to the mall. I looked out the window at the stinking grey billows undulating from the orifices of industrial smokestacks in the distance, like ominous fog from a fissuring mountaintop. God on Mount Sinai.

I had a plan, and God knew it.

The mall had a record store. The record store was my connection to culture—the leathery rock and roll glitz of whatever was playing on MTV in the early '90s. I had a twenty-dollar bill. It was tucked inside a birthday card from my grandmother, Mimi, and

I'd stowed it in my chain wallet for the occasion. I was going to buy an album, but my parents couldn't know about it. The protective Christian bubble over our domestic world would never knowingly allow this particular CD into my Sony Walkman. Somehow, I had to break away, make the purchase, stow it in my oversized jeans, and return to the family fold as if carrying no ill-gotten gains to speak of. My family crossed the mall's threshold, excited to browse and shop together, enjoy a food court dinner.

"What about you, Josh?" my mom asked. "Which stores would you like to visit?" She was smiling, oblivious to my scheming.

"Actually," I said, "can I go to the arcade for a bit while you guys shop?"

My parents looked disappointed but conceded. I watched them shrink into a department store. My heart racing, I set off toward Blockbuster Music, Sheryl Crow's "All I Wanna Do" issuing from the mall speakers, soundtracking my covert scheme. Then it was in my hands, the illicit material itself. Parental advisory, explicit lyrics. The low-stakes theater of adolescence. Maybe, I thought, I could remove the warning, then I wouldn't have to hide the purchase from my parents. But no, why did I need to sneak away to buy it when I'd said I'd be at the arcade? I rolled the twenty, rough to the touch, between my fingertips and took a deep breath. Parental advisory, explicit lyrics.

I imagined, for a moment, a world without the secret. A world in which I might sit with my father, unafraid, and tell him what I liked about the album—a world in which the album wasn't a secret at all. And maybe he'd never like it himself, but maybe he'd get it, this man who had been a teenager in the '70s, with long shaggy hair, Aerosmith exploding from the stereo in his bedroom, his father—my grandfather—glowering his disapproval.

I bought the record. Somewhere in the distance, smoke and sulfur went on swirling into the humid Savannah darkness.

PREFACE TO ACT I

HOW CHRISTIANS DESTROY ART

I HAVE NO IDEA how it actually happened, but I have to assume the guy made a mess. It was all the way back in 1987. Photographer Andres Serrano submerged a small, plastic crucifix in a glass tank filled with his own urine. On the cross hung the familiar figure of Jesus, his impaled hands outstretched in misery. Serrano took a picture. He called it, *Immersion (Piss Christ).*

It's not something I've ever done—steeped something in a jar of pee just to take a picture of it—but I assume you can't go peeing in a jar, dropping trinkets in it, then retrieving them without spillage. If you want to be an artist, you've got to make sacrifices, I guess. If you're going to make people as upset as he did, you might as well work for it.

More than twenty years later, four individuals wearing sunglasses entered a French museum carrying a hammer inside a sock. They made a different kind of mess.

Between those two moments—the one with the jar of urine and the one with the hammer inside a sock—*Piss Christ* had become the subject of predictable, ongoing outrage. Former United States Senator Alphonse D'Amato called the photograph "shocking, abhorrent and completely undeserving of any recognition whatsoever."[1] In 1997, the Catholic Archbishop of Melbourne was so bothered by it that he sought an injunction from the Supreme Court of Victoria to stop *Piss Christ* from being displayed in Australia's most visited art museum.

Then, after all those years and protests, four individuals in sunglasses entered a French exhibition where *Piss Christ* was displayed. It was Palm Sunday, a day when Christians remember Jesus's celebrated entry into Jerusalem before he was executed. The four visitors in sunglasses assaulted the guards on duty, drew a hammer from a sock, and in the ensuing scuffle, managed to smash the Plexiglas that protected *Piss Christ* before using a sharp implement to slash the photograph beyond repair. Their work complete, the vandals fled the scene. When the press wrote about it, they called the criminals "Christian protestors." This is one way that Christians destroy art, but not the only way. They do it all the time.

The French gallery was eventually re-opened with the destroyed artwork on display just as it had been before Palm Sunday. The newly modified *Piss Christ* became an inadvertently poignant spectacle. The alleged Christian criminals had (by intention or co-incidence) driven their angry hammer directly into Jesus's face. Blemished by a violent crater, the visage of Christ erupted with splintering fissures and shattered glass. It was just as the prophet Isaiah had predicted: there were many who were appalled at him— his appearance was so disfigured beyond that of any human being and his form marred beyond human likeness.[2]

Following the incident on Palm Sunday, Andres Serrano—the art-ist responsible for *Immersion (Piss Christ)*—described the indig-nation constantly circling his piece like an angry buzzard as "a misinterpretation." He said, "I am a Christian, and a Christian art-ist."[3] What does it mean to be a Christian artist? If Serrano is a Christian artist, does that make *Piss Christ* a Christian work of art? If so, why would other Christians want to destroy it?

When beholding *Piss Christ*, another Christian—Catholic nun, Sister Wendy Beckett—found the image powerful and moving, deriving from it a strong sense of conviction. "I thought [Serrano] was saying… this is what we are doing to Christ. We are not treat-ing him with reverence… We live very vulgar lives. We put Christ in a bottle of urine—in practice. It was a very admonitory work… But I think to call it blasphemous is really rather begging the ques-tion: it could be, or it could not be. It is what you make of it, and I could make something that made me feel a deep desire to reverence the death of Christ *more* by this suggestion that this is what, in practice, the world is doing."[4] Sister Wendy saw the same photo as the Christian vandals and, like them, found it vulgar. But, in Sister Mary's mind, the spectator is reprimanded by the vulgarity of the piece. The vulgar life, which treats the sacrifice of Jesus with contempt, also desecrates that sacrifice. It puts Jesus in a jar of urine.

Others interpreted the image of Jesus submerged in urine as a commentary on the cheapening of sacred symbols. The domestication of the crucifix. Instrument of torture as decorative flourish. "The thing about the crucifix itself is that we treat it almost like a fashion accessory. When you see it, you're not horrified by it at all, but what it represents is the crucifixion of a man," Serrano said of his work. "So if *Piss Christ* upsets you, maybe it's a good thing to think about what happened on the cross."[5]

But the image is more than its ideological agenda. As a moment captured by a camera and committed to film, formal qualities of style, composition, and lighting factor in how it is beheld and understood. Art critic Lucy Lippard admired the piece, calling it a "darkly beautiful photographic image... The small wood and plastic crucifix becomes virtually monumental as it floats, photographically enlarged, in a deep rosy glow that is both ominous and glorious."[6] What, if anything, does the shape and hue of the *Piss Christ* have to do with what it does or doesn't mean to say? If you follow the paper trail, *Piss Christ* seems to mostly (or only) upset people who claim to be Christians, and that on the basis of their Christianity itself. But *Piss Christ* was created by someone who describes himself as a Christian artist. Some Christians argued that *Piss Christ* created in them a deep desire to regard Jesus with more reverence, not less. That it compelled them to worship. For them, it was the ugliness of the image that somehow instilled reverence, though others beholding the same image regarded its visual composition—apart from its theological implications—as not ugly, but "beautiful" and "glorious."

Does *Piss Christ* go too far to make a point unsurprisingly lost on most of its audience? Is such a notoriously offensive image defensible? If this work is indeed blasphemous in any way, is it wrong for Christians to look at it? To admire it? If the artist *had* intended to defile the image of Jesus with his work, would Sister Wendy Beckett be wrong to infer from the image a meaning the artist did not intend and be drawn to worship just the same? Given the unavoidably incendiary nature of the image and its title, does the artist owe the audience an explanation? After all, if he is a Christian, and if the work is potentially blasphemous, shouldn't he clear the air, lest some of his fellow Christians be led astray? And really, is a work of art really worth all this controversy? If Andres Serrano had wanted to make a statement about the vulgar cheapening of Jesus's sacrifice, why not do it in a way less likely to attract protesters with hammers? With a title like *Piss Christ,* anyone could have foreseen scandal on the horizon, especially a Christian.

This is a book about all those things.

Some people who read this book might be artists and art enthusiasts. The painters, the musicians, the novelists, the sculptors, designers, illustrators, filmmakers, singers, dancers, and on down the
list. Some readers, by wiring or nature or upbringing or happen-
stance, deeply admire the craft, though they may not be artists
themselves. For both the artist and art enthusiast, the arts are in-
dispensable—an important and necessary means through which
they process reality. For them, vocation, calling, and even identity
itself are all irrevocably tethered to art and creativity.

But maybe some people who read this book think of themselves
as unfriendly to the arts. Hostile to them. For them, art is, at best,
inessential and at worst, dangerous, misleading, and destructive.
But most of the people reading this book probably sit somewhere
between the two extremes, leaning toward enthusiast or cynic, depending on context and genre. For them, art is not a way of life,
per se, but it is fine and good. They enjoy music playing in their
cars, streaming movies and miniseries, even decorative flourishes
in their homes. Maybe they've been particularly moved by something creative from time to time, and they can certainly imagine
the same thing happening to someone else. If you are the minority
fixed at either pole—the art enthusiast or deprecator—most of the

people you know are in the middle: Enthusiastic, indifferent, or cynical. Depending.

Within that wide spectrum, there are Christians. There are disciples of Jesus who love art, who create art, who need art. There are disciples of Jesus who regard art with skepticism or contempt. There are disciples of Jesus who don't think of themselves as art lovers or haters, who haven't really given it a lot of thought one way or another. And, like many, they lean to either extreme from time to time. One Christian might find themselves in profound awe of art and creativity when hearing a beautiful worship song. That same Christian might, however, find themselves skeptical and disapproving of the arts when beholding *Piss Christ*. This is a book for all of you.

For every one of us, art is inescapable. Today, you will be inundated with visuals, designs, screens, music, video, and photographs. You will wear clothes, use furniture, eat food, behold advertisements that—good or bad, well-made or shoddy—were all birthed from some creative process. Though our access to art and the mediums for creating it have evolved over time, art and creativity are not new. They are as old as anything can possibly be.

And almost as old as art itself is the way we destroy it.

ACT I:
WHAT
IS ART?

CHAPTER 1:1

PLATO, PICASSO, AND A GUY
THAT PAINTS WITH BLOOD

MIDWAY THROUGH A NEARLY four-hour performance, a bull carcass emerges.

In the midst of what has already been a spectacularly grotesque scene, a nude performer fixed to a cross is set against the carcass. A dissonant organ blares. Somewhere, a whistle is blown, signaling frenzied performers to dive into the animal remains, tearing at blood-soaked entrails and an avalanche of wet tomatoes and grapes. The whistle blows again, and the performers pause, panting. Another whistle and the chaos resumes. All this happens in Austrian artist Hermann Nitsch's performance piece, *150.Action*. I did the research writing this book and the videos and stills grossed me out, like I could smell it. A day after the show, Nitsch reportedly explained to an audience discussion panel that "many people understand my work, many people don't. That's normal."[1] But Nitsch's creative output isn't all whistles and animal guts. He also paints. With blood. Asked about his preferred material, Nitsch replied, "Some choose paint, I choose blood."[2]

Okay. Sure.

Herman Nitsch is one example among many artists to divide audiences. His work elicits predictable revulsion alongside glowing acclaim. The controversial press surrounding one of his galleries—much like the protests outside one of his events—is a hotbed of debate over sexuality, animal rights, and what even qualifies as art in the first place. Maybe defining art at all seems hopelessly abstract, but all of us knowingly or unknowingly maintain some rubric by which we define what *is* and is *not* art. Sometimes, it takes a guy filling bull carcasses with grapes to force our paradigm out of hiding.

ART THEORY (IN PASSING)

In her book *But is it art?* Cynthia Freeland laments, "A big problem in laying out the data for this book is that our term 'art' might not even apply in many cultures or eras."[3] The truth is, there has never been a uniform consensus on what does and does not qualify as art. There are helpful ideas, terms, and theories as to why one might intend a given thing as a work of art, or why one might experience a thing as if it is art. When I started writing this thing, I told a guy I know—a professor—about it. "Give it up," he said. "Defining art. It can't be done." I disagree. So here we are.

Classical tragedy—a form of drama heavy on human suffering—

originated in sixth century BCE in Athens. Ancient discussions of these plays produced something called the imitation theory: Art *imitates* what one experiences in life and the world. The Greek philosopher Aristotle believed such a thing was viable for entertainment and educational purposes. Okay, so art imitates life. There were, however, limits to Aristotle's approval.

The 431 BC play *Madea*, for example, tells the story of a woman who murders her own children as well as the new bride and father-in-law of her unfaithful husband. (For the latter two, she employs a magical flesh-melting robe.) The whole thing ends with Madea riding off in the chariot of the sun-god Helios. All this to the chagrin of Aristotle, who believed that depicting a protagonist who knowingly does evil was wrong. He would likely take similar issue with an illustration from 330 BC, which is today displayed in the Louvre: Madea, gripping her small child by the hair as she drives a blade into his side, little brush dabs of red raining from the wound like blood confetti.

Sure, these events may imitate life in some sense, but to what good end? Aristotle defended the idea of dramatic tragedies with moral characters. He figured if a tragedy depicts a good character that confronts the hardships of existence and it's done with technical precision and excellent craftsmanship, an audience might leave better for it. But not, he believed, if a character does evil without clear consequence. Aristotle's disdain for moral ambiguity is alive and well today. Many modern filmgoers, readers, and music enthusiasts have little patience for art with no explicit moral compass.

Alright, well, art imitates life but should be, in some sense… moral?

Aristotle's teacher, Plato, on the other hand, couldn't be bothered with tragedies and didn't seem to regard sculpture, painting, pottery, or architecture as "art" so much as simple craftsmanship. A tragedy, like a painting, only imitates things already in the physical world, which, according to Plato, was not as real or true as the eternal non-physical world, so why bother? Besides, a play like *Madea* only clouds the judgment of its audience, as it fails to teach what Plato believed to be "eternal virtues." Plato had a very low view of art, which he understood as appealing to the imagination and, thus, little more than a distraction from a greater spiritual reality. Plato's deficient view of art lives on. Many modern spectators insist on ham-fisted literalism in art or that art focus only and entirely on some unambiguous spiritual reality.

So, wait, art should do more than morally imitate life? It should address the *non-physical* nature of existence instead?

It doesn't take a Greek philosopher to spot the holes in imitation theory. A variety of entire genres— surrealism, expressionism, impressionism, and abstract art—are unconcerned with imitating the formal reality of life in the physical world. If we concede that art doesn't always imitate life in the strictest sense, we're not any closer to figuring out what it is or what it does.

For many, art is about beauty. Thomas Aquinas was uninterested in art as an imitation. Instead, he argued that human works of art tap into the nature of God. More precisely, God is beautiful, so art should follow suit. Aquinas and his medieval peers were more concerned with theology than art theory proper, but their theology of beauty is evident in everything from their writing to the construction of their cathedrals, and you can find tons of people who still agree with Aquinas today. Even well-meaning efforts to recapture creativity in the Christian tradition often emphasize the alleged centrality of beauty.

Right. So, art is about making beautiful things? But what qualifies as beautiful? Who decides?

For Scottish philosopher David Hume, the discussion of aesthetics—the unique qualities of a given work—was a question of taste. It doesn't seem like Hume would have liked Herman Nitsch's blood paintings. Hume believed it was important to distinguish between whether we *like* something and whether that work is *actually good*. Art, he argued, should echo the values of the Enlightenment—upright morality and forward-thinking. Only educated and experienced individuals, Hume believed, could identify a universal "standard of taste." Under the qualified scrutiny of the elite, Nitsch's bloodied canvases would likely not pass for decent art or as art at all. *Liking* something is subjective and mostly beyond your control, while value, for Hume, is objective. If you like blood paintings, it doesn't make them good. If you don't like traditional fine art, it doesn't make traditional fine art bad.

So, scratch all that; art *is* about beauty, but only as defined by those qualified to designate what is and is not beautiful? Many people still argue as much.

Another German philosopher, Immanuel Kant, agreed with Hume that taste was objective—that one work of art could be inarguably better than another. But unlike Hume, Kant believed the quality of art depended more on the piece itself rather than the qualifications of the one beholding it. Lots of people seem to agree on the beauty of something like a sunset or a symphony, and that's because, Kant argued, they really are, objectively, beautiful. People of taste, he thought, recognize this, and our understanding of beauty is informed by their broad consensus.

So, art is about objective beauty, on which most people agree? The herd—the *classy* herd—becomes the arbiter of true art. Popular = good. So, is art about life or morality or spirituality only? Is art necessarily beautiful? Is that beauty defined by the elite or the majority? Forget all of that. All of it. It's a mess.

In all the tangled squabbles over what qualifies as art, some prefer to set clarifying semantics aside and simply enjoy the art, whatever it is. Because art *communicates* something. According to something called cognitive theory, art communicates complicated thoughts and ideas—not unlike words. So, Dr. Seuss's book, *Yertle the Turtle*, communicates ideas about Adolph Hitler. Neil Blomkamp's film *District 9* communicates ideas about xenophobia and apartheid South Africa. But another take, expression theory, disagrees, arguing that art communicates *feelings* more than it does thoughts or ideas—it makes us react emotionally with a smile, laughter, a gasp, sigh, a scream.

The great Russian novelist Leo Tolstoy summarizes expression theory in his essay *What is Art?*. He argues that the purpose of art is to "evoke in oneself a feeling one has once experienced and having evoked it in oneself then by means of movements, lines, colours, sounds, or forms expressed in words, so to transmit this feeling that others experience the same feeling."[4] But there's a problem. Tolstoy believed that to transmit a feeling, the artist must have experienced it themselves. You can find lots of people who still agree. At the time of writing, a common outrage motif in the entertainment industry is the question of who is allowed to tell what stories. Can a White filmmaker make a movie about a Black family? Can someone who is not autistic write a novel about someone who is?

Must an artist really have personal familiarity with a given feeling or idea to communicate or comment on it with their art? Should we discredit *Rocky* because Sylvester Stallone, the film's star and screenwriter, was not a boxer? Did the Greek playwright Euripides require any personal experience of adultery or infanticide to imbue *Medea* with emotional resonance? The 1955 novel *Lolita* features a middle-aged narrator who becomes sexually obsessed with a 12-year-old girl. This does not mean that author Vladimir Nabokov was a pedophile. And really, anyone taking *Medea* or *Lolita* seriously would likely agree that the most significant among the ideas and emotions communicated by these works are the ones abstracted from the surface. *Rocky* is about more than boxing. *Madea* is not just about a crazy lady with a magical flesh-melting robe. It's also about loneliness, isolation, and betrayal as much (or more so) as it is about murder and revenge.

Only an unfortunate few have experienced adultery, and even fewer express the pain they experience in its wake with vengeful violence against children. But most humans know what it means to feel betrayed, to crave retribution even at the expense of moral dignity. And who knows which of these emotional messages Euripides, the play's author, *intended* to communicate in *Medea*, or to what end, anyway? Sure, he may have said so at one point or another, but if his intention contradicts the audience's experience, is the audience's experience nullified? Philosopher Nicholas Wolterstorff defines artistic excellence as what happens when a work of art accomplishes the purpose for which it was created.[5]

What happens if we experience something else?

I SEE A PARASITE

Different people experience art differently. That's good. In the *Seinfeld* episode "The Letter," an elderly art-loving couple admires an oil painting of the show's eccentric character, Cosmo Kramer. "I sense great vulnerability," the woman gushes. "A man-child crying out for love. An innocent orphan in the post-modern world."[6]

The man disagrees. "I see a parasite. A sexually depraved miscreant who is seeking only to gratify his basest and most immediate urges."[7]

When an artist doesn't say much about an intended message in their work, audiences and critics tend to argue about it, arriving at different conclusions and emphasizing them with passionate fervor. Ask someone about Stanley Kubrick's 1980 film *The Shining*. Some wholeheartedly believe that it's about the slaughter of Native Americans. Others, the Holocaust. For others still, *The Shining* is about Kubrick's involvement in faking the moon landing. Even without all the subtext, no one seems to agree on how to interpret the movie's *surface* narrative, not to mention how it ends. Maybe Kubrick didn't have any of these things in mind making *The Shining*.

In his book, *On Writing*, author Stephen King admits to having no preconceived symbolism in mind while drafting his debut novel, *Carrie*. "When I read *Carrie* over prior to starting the second draft, I noticed there was blood at all three crucial points of the story… It seemed to mean something. That meaning wasn't consciously created, however."[8] King, the artist at the helm, had not *deliberately* woven a symbolic motif into *Carrie* via the image of blood, and yet, there it was. He then realized the resonance of all this blood imagery was powerful and varied. "Blood is strongly linked to the idea of sacrifice; for young women it's associated with reaching physical maturity and the ability to bear children; in the Christian religion (plenty of others, as well), it's symbolic of both sin and salvation."[9] Any of these blood symbols, King noted, might imbue the story of *Carrie* with layered meaning. Some of them you grab by skimming the surface, others on repeated readings, and some only if they are conjured up by the unique perspective and experience of the reader. In each case, the message is received in the reader's thinking and feeling. That's how it works. Harvard professor Nelson Goodman argued for this duality of thought and feeling in his book *Languages of Art*. He wrote, "What we know through art is felt in our bones and nerves and muscles as well as grasped by our minds."[10]

WHAT ART IS/DOES

People have been arguing about what qualifies as art for thousands of years, but there are elements of truth in most theories. In simplest terms, when a person or people create something that communicates ideas, emotions, or craftsmanship, this is art. That's about it.

The mediums, materials, and forms through which one accomplishes this are almost limitless. Paintings, sculptures, cathedrals, carvings, drawings, photographs, symphonies, novels, poems, plays, songs, and films are obvious examples. But a sentence might be a work of art. A found object repurposed in a new context. A public fast. A dissonant drone. A comic book. Even a canvas spattered with animal blood.

Art communicates—intentionally or unintentionally, it doesn't really matter. Art elicits a response in the audience's thinking or feeling or both. That response might seem superficial (entertainment, a chuckle, cheap sentimentality) or profound (grief, hope, existential horror). To pull this off, art can imitate life, but it doesn't have to. Art can achieve its communicative purpose to an overtly beautiful, positive, moral, or uplifting end, but it doesn't have to do that either. Art can utilize beauty to say something beautiful, or something ugly to say something beautiful, or something beautiful to say something ugly. And the "something" that art says might be beautiful or ugly depending, on who you ask.

Art is obviously complex, but it's more than that. Art is transcendent—inarguably fundamental to the human experience across time and culture for *all people*. And it's always been this way because God made it up.

To take issue with art is to take issue with God. To devalue art is to devalue God.

CHAPTER 1:2

GALAXIES AND BLUE POMEGRANATES

THE FIRST LINE IN the Bible is about God:

בְּרֵאשִׁית, בָּרָא אֱלֹהִים, אֵת הַשָּׁמַיִם, וְאֵת הָאָרֶץ

In the beginning God created the heaven and the earth.

This singular, compact sentence begins the story of the Bible in all its epic, sprawling, complex glory. Already, we've been introduced to the story's protagonist. Already, we know something fundamental about who the protagonist is. God creates. God is creative. One of the first things we learn from the Bible about the personhood of God is that God is an artist.

What comes to mind when you read the word *artist*? For some, the word itself is a pretentious moniker reserved for self-important blowhards. Say, "I'm an artist," and watch people roll their eyes. An artist is likely entitled and work-shy, flighty, someone who refuses to get a real job. Others lean hard into the other extreme: An artist is a mystic. The only kind of person with any worthwhile perspective or cultural currency. A gnostic sage rising high above the rabble of non-creative lesser-thans, third eye wide open. But long before stereotypes and misconceptions, the author of Genesis began the masterful saga of the Bible with words that would challenge, comfort, and confound billions of humans for thousands of years: In the beginning, God *created*. God is an artist.

THE FIRST ACTS OF CREATIVITY

The first chronicle of God's creativity across the opening pages of Genesis is hotly debated. But when you strip away arguments about dinosaurs and evolution, you still have a very clear story about God's artistry. In it, God orders and forms from watery chaos a garden overflowing with life and beauty. From the raw materials of disorder, God crafts something new. And this new thing is ordered, beautiful, and good. On this, all Christians agree, regardless of your particular theory of how God created or exactly how long it took him to do it.

In the story, God does a lot of creative work. Then, like a painter taking a few steps backward to behold the fruits of his labor, "God saw all that he had made, and it was very good."[1] Some of the things God creates are wonderfully pragmatic; others seem to exist simply because it is lovely or interesting for them to exist. God creates things that are useful, ornamental, specifically purposeful, or just kind of neat. There are things in the natural world with profound theological significance that make wonderful scientific sense—like reproduction, or opposable thumbs, or photosynthesis. Other created things are explainable in a certain sense, but they are marked by wonderful and extravagant artistic flourishes, like sunsets, peacocks, the cosmic glow of stars, the way your breath escapes as an ethereal vapor in the cold. Biologist Jeff Ploegstra argues, "It may seem odd coming from a biologist, but I think we should be studying the creation first and foremost as a work of art."[2]

Because of the imagery it evokes, it's easy to think of Genesis as this primordial document somehow written as a real-time commentary on a very young cosmos, but it wasn't. Scholar John Sailhammer theorizes that the author may have assembled Genesis from a variety of existing stories—written down or transmitted via oral tradition—adding his own narrative touches along the way. This volume may not have been edited until a few thousand years later.[3] Genesis was born into and circulated throughout a world not unlike ours in its disagreement over how the universe came into being, who was responsible, and what role humanity played in the whole thing, if any. Certain aspects of the story comment on or even rebut competing ancient Near Eastern creation myths. In the Genesis story, the grand finale of God's creative symphony is the ordination of human beings. During the brainstorming phase of the project, God says, "Let us make mankind in our image."[4] In Hebrew, the word *image* is *tselem* (צֶלֶם). It often refers to the statues commissioned by ancient Near Eastern kings to represent the king's likeness to his royal subjects. Or it might reference the carved images of gods in the ancient world displayed in temples for the sake of their worshipers. This is what the gods look like. Knowing this, the ancient reader of Genesis would have noticed that the author disagrees with kingly statues and idols. In Genesis, *humans* are the "image of God."[5] Human beings are appointed by God to reveal to the world what the invisible God is like.

What does it mean for human beings to be made in God's image? Humanity will act as the likeness of God in their ruling and stewardship of God's Creation. But the idea isn't that human beings are the Parks and Rec Department of Eden. We don't merely oversee God's work of art; we partner with God in the further development of creation.

Hebrew scholar Tim Mackie describes this task by saying that humans "rule the earth by cultivating it… By harnessing all of the earth's raw potential and then making something more and new out of it."[6] That's pretty broad. Create families, communities, neighborhoods, and cities. It's about gardening, agriculture, plant and animal husbandry. Create culture, peace, work, business, goodness. From what is often called *the cultural mandate* of Genesis, we build our theology of work, vocation, ecology, environmentalism and animal welfare. And it's more than the practical expansion of the human project. This is an invitation to *create*.

God begins an expansive, breathtaking work of art, but it isn't finished. In the story, he invites humans into his studio and hands them a paintbrush. Of course, if you know the story, things kind of go off the rails by the time you get to chapter three. Humanity is led astray by a lie, deciding it would be better if God weren't in charge of this whole creative collaboration project. The rest of the Bible is about the lengths to which God will go to rescue people from their own foolishness and the lengths to which people will go to avoid being rescued.

But in the dramatic oscillation of the Bible's unfolding narrative, the cultural mandate is never repealed. The world is broken, marred by sin, suffering, and death, but we're still responsible for taking it somewhere. God still wants us as partners. God continues to invite us into his creativity.

GOD AS ART PARTON

In Exodus 25, Moses is talking to God on Mount Sinai when God declares that Israel is to build a special tent to house his presence among them.[7] What follows are seven detailed chapters that describe exactly how this tent is to be constructed, furnished, and decorated. Here, God's extravagant artistry is on full display—not by speaking galaxies into existence as it was at the beginning of the story, but through woodworking, sculpture, and painting. God is commanding and encouraging a very *human* artistic endeavor.

Of course, God could have crafted his own dwelling place. A more impressive one, I'm sure. Instead, God appoints human artists and gives them instructions. Inside the tent, God wants flowers, fruit, gold, angels. Each image is pregnant with symbolism, drawing Israel (and the reader of Exodus) back to the Garden of Eden—the first story of God's creative artistry.

Included in these chapters are patterns for outfits to be worn by priests working in the Tabernacle. God says, "Make pomegranates of blue, purple and scarlet yarn around the hem of the robe, with gold bells between them."[8] Pomegranates, in nature, are red or purple but not blue. God's design includes decorative flourishes— what we often call "artistic liberties." Long before Aristotle or the imitation theory of art, God dabbled in surrealism—conceiving visual feats of artistry that contradict reality in strange and beautiful ways. Divorced of context, the intricacies of the Tabernacle read as if they spool out from God's unending attention to and obsession with insignificant detail. But as with any great work of art, the artist is up to something. The seemingly endless details of the Tabernacle belong to a story in which God promises to restore access to his presence—access that had been forfeited to humanity's evil. The tabernacle itself—blue pomegranates and all—is an expression of that promise. One way God chooses to express the beauty of his faithfulness is in beautiful, surreal art. The instructions for the tabernacle—the detailed visuals, the symbols, the priestly outfits—though lengthy and specific, showcase God's creative genius and his fatherly affection for Israel. Like a dad who spends time fashioning a special gift for his child, God is pouring over every small detail so that the goodness of his craftsmanship and artistic intent might pair perfectly with his generous love. In Exodus 31, we learn that God specially appointed two men as artists.

> Then the Lord said to Moses, "See, I have chosen Bezalel son of Uri, the son of Hur, of the tribe of Judah, and I have filled him with the Spirit of God, with wisdom, with understanding, with knowledge and with all kinds of skills—to make artistic designs for work in gold, silver and bronze, to cut and set stones, to work in wood, and to engage in all kinds of crafts. Moreover, I have appointed Oholiab son of Ahisamak, of the tribe of Dan, to help him. Also I have given ability to all the skilled workers to make everything I have commanded you. (Exodus 31v1-6)

From this simple stretch of details, we learn that God *commissions artists*. God doesn't want Moses to do the artwork because Moses isn't that kind of artist. But God does want it done. He commands it. He wants it to be done *well,* "skillfully," not by just anyone, but by an artist.[9] God could accomplish all of this some other way (or not at all), but God wants art, commands it, commissions it, and—

like any artist— takes the way it is done very seriously.

"BIBLICAL" ART

Later in the Hebrew Scriptures, God commissions the building of a Temple with the same concern for artistic detail. Once again, there are instructions, and once again, we're told explicitly that God made them up.[24] But God doesn't restrict his commissioned artists to follow his instructions with slavish rigidity. He leaves many things creatively non-specific. What exactly do cherubim look like? What exactly is the pattern of the colorful priestly robe? The artist will decide using their God-given imagination, creativity, and skill.

This is important to God for an atmosphere of worship. Even notoriously stringent and grumpy-sounding theologian John Calvin argued, "It was not enough for the faithful, in those days, to depend upon the Word of God, and to engage in those ceremonial services which he required, unless, aided by *external* symbols, they *elevated* their *minds* above these, and yielded to God *spiritual* worship. God, indeed, gave real tokens of his presence in that visible sanctuary, but not for the purpose of binding the senses and thoughts of his people to earthly elements; he wished rather that these *external* symbols serve as *ladders*, by which the faithful might *ascend* even to heaven."[10]

Symbols are important to God. He doesn't even mind if the Bible's authors use wild creative metaphors and anthropomorphism to describe him. God *inspires* them to do exactly that. Thus, in passages like Leviticus 20v6 and Numbers 6v25, God has a "face." God the Father doesn't have a physical face; these descriptions are artistic liberties. The same is true of Exodus 7v5's claim that God has hands or Psalm 89v10's suggestion that he has arms. Elsewhere, God has eyes and feet. Nostrils. Rides on a cloud. Cries tears. God is a shepherd, a doctor, the owner of a vineyard. Jesus is a vine, he's a husband, a mother hen, a lion, then a lamb. God's Spirit is like water, or a dove, or wind. These word pictures beautifully capture true things about God with creative language that isn't "true" in the *literal* sense but is very true in the *figurative* sense. It's beautifully poetic. It's art.

In fact, a third of the entire Bible is poetry. There is more poetry in the Bible than explicit discourse. Tim Mackie observes, "The majority of God's speech in the Bible is represented as poetry."[11] When God talks, he's a poet. When his human authors record his voice, to them, it's like poetry. Throughout the story, Biblical characters often break from a narrative in progress to recite historically rich and theologically complex songs, and the Bible's biggest collection of poetry proper is the Psalms. Most of the Bible's readers know this, but many of those same readers don't realize that the Psalms were designed as a compendium of poetry for Israel in exile. Before Babylon invaded Israel and destroyed Jerusalem, the worship of God's people was anchored in a specific setting. Ancient Jewish people would enter the Temple (like the Tabernacle before it) to be absolutely surrounded by vivid imagery. There were priestly rituals, candles burning, ever-present sounds of prayers and songs. It was an immersive sensory experience designed to cultivate a sense of God's story and proximity. But when the Babylonians laid siege to Jerusalem, they all but demolished the Temple. Cut off from the land, how would Israel enter their place of worship? Through poems that recreate the vivid imagery and symbolism of a virtual Temple.

Through art.

The authors of the Bible understand art as a means by which humans can immerse themselves in God's presence and engage in deep, meaningful worship. There's a Hebrew word ("נָוָה") that English Bibles often translate as "exalt." Literally, it means to *beautify*. "Yahweh is my God, I will *beautify* him with my praises." God is already the origin and source of all beauty, yet somehow, we can *beautify* him with words, lyrics, songs. With *art*.

From the first line of the first story in all the Scriptures all the way to the closing pages of Revelation, God is depicted as an artist inviting others to create, admire, and experience art. God meets humanity in art, and humanity enters into the presence of God himself through art.

Given that beauty is such a prominent concern in God's work, we might be tempted to agree with Thomas Aquinas: Art taps into beauty as one fundamental aspect of God's nature. God is beautiful, art done rightly follows suit.

But I'm not sure it's that simple.

CHAPTER 1:3

BEAUTIFULLY UGLY AND
UNNECESSARILY COMPLICATED

YOU'RE TAKING A STROLL through an urban metropolitan area one afternoon when you happen upon a small crowd and a foul smell. The center of the hubbub is a disheveled man lying on the ground, bound by constricting rope so that he can barely move. Before him burns a small fire—the source of the fetid odor. On the fire, a loaf of dark bread and in the fire itself, excrement. Moved by compassion, you kneel to free the man from his bonds. Someone in the crowd stops you.

"He did this to himself," they say.

"He's been at this for days," someone else observes. "Supposedly, some kind of statement about injustice and idolatry," they sigh, rolling their eyes.

Another person snorts their disapproval. "Give me a break." One by one, they turn and walk away.

So goes the story of Ezekiel. In a series of increasingly bizarre feats of street theater, Ezekiel spends more than a year lying on his side, bound by rope. God commands him to prepare food over human feces, and when Ezekiel laments the impurity of the whole thing, God allows him to substitute cow droppings instead. Ezekiel cuts his hair with a sword and burns it. He even prepares a scale model of Jerusalem, then dramatizes an attack on the tiny city like a kid playing Godzilla. No one is into it. Everyone thinks he's a hack. But none of it was Ezekiel's idea. God told him to do it. Each specific detail. God commissions bizarre and offensive performance art.

In 1974, Yugoslav artist Marina Abramović performed a six-hour piece in which she stood motionless, inviting an audience to interact with her using any of 72 objects arranged on a nearby table. There were innocuous things—a feather, a flower, some grapes. But there was also a scalpel, some nails, and a handgun loaded with a single bullet. The evening began with calm curiosity, but in a few hours the participants became increasingly violent and unhinged. Someone finally intervened when one audience member put the loaded gun to Abramović's head, forcing her to work her own finger around the trigger. When the six hours concluded, the gallery announced that the performance had ended. Abramović finally stirred. She later commented on the way the audience fled the exhibit to avoid having to confront her, this woman who had moments prior been little more than an object.

Abramović's piece, *Rhythm 0*, was intended for more than head-lines and shock value. *Rhythm 0* continues to spark conversation around latent human depravity and the objectification of women. Could the same ideas be broached without the elaborate perfor-mance art? Without the handgun and the assault? Probably. But Marina Abramović harnessed her God-given creativity to con-ceive of and carry out the performance of *Rhythm 0,* and *Rhythm 0* was effective. Similarly, one could argue that God was entirely capable of getting his message across without prophetic perfor-mance art involving swords and fire and cow dung. But given a choice between shocking performance art and no shocking perfor-mance art, God chose shocking performance art. What does that say about God?

"Exposición N° 1" was another controversial art exhibit by Guillermo Vargas. The show included a live dog, visibly malnour-ished and tied to a wall by a short length of rope. "You are what you read" was written in dog food on the wall behind the animal. Internet rumors of the dog's mistreatment and alleged death stirred international outrage, which Vargas claimed to be an extension of the piece. The dog had reportedly been discovered on the streets of Nicaragua in a state of abject neglect but failed to rouse the concern of onlookers until it was displayed in an art gallery.

It was said of "Exposición N° 1" (and of many controversial works of art) that the shocking nature of the piece distracted the audience from its intended message. This is likely true from time to time. The same could be said of a prophet who burns his hair in a fire stoked with feces. Weren't there more precise, less grotesque ways to comment on Israel's rebellion? Absolutely. But God is an artist. Ezekiel's "sign acts"—though designed by God—are not beautiful in any traditional sense. They're ugly. They aren't up-lifting, and ultimately, they weren't redemptive. These pieces powerfully communicate a bleak—even obscene—meditation on and critique of Israel's injustice and worship of other gods. And the whole thing is in the Bible.

The narrative is alive with God's expressive passion and outrage against evil. God never expresses any concern for whether or not his art might be offensive or misunderstood. In fact, by the time you get to Ezekiel chapter 5—after God's strange and distasteful performance parables—we learn that God already realizes the per-formances won't "work." Israel will not take Ezekiel's symbolic warnings seriously, and Jerusalem will be destroyed.

God commissions the performance art anyway.

Even the way God appears to Ezekiel is a swirl of wild, imagina-tive visuals. Rather than dialoguing with Ezekiel through a boom-ing heavenly voice or through a series of thoughts deposited into

Ezekiel's mind, God shows up in powerful images. Ezekiel describes a royal throne chariot made up of living humanoid creatures, each with multiple faces and wings. The four wheels of the chariot defy the laws of physics. These undulating, otherworldly entities atop their strange system of locomotion support a throne. On it, an incredible being of sapphire and flame. Ezekiel calls it, "the appearance of the likeness of the glory of Yahweh."[1] Then, and only after all that aesthetic pageantry, God starts talking. God appears to Ezekiel through fantastic and surreal imagery. Ezekiel recognizes these visuals as both the likeness and glory of God. When God finally speaks, he commands *more* strange and provocative imagery, this time through Ezekiel's performance art parables, though God knows the meaning will be lost on most of the audience.

If that doesn't sound like an artist, I don't know what does.

TRUMPETS AND ANIMAL BLOOD

The eighth album from the experimental rock band The Flaming Lips is called *Zaireeka*. Packaged as four unique compact discs, *Zaireeka* is designed for simultaneous playback across four distinct audio systems. If you manage to synchronize such an event, the result is a strange symphonic foray into melody and noise. I arranged a *Zaireeka* listening party once. A friend mocked the effort—four of us hunched over our own boomboxes, desperately coordinating the playback of each track, one by one. "This thing is so pretentious," my friend snorted. "So self-indulgent."

In 1 Chronicles 23, David tasks four thousand Israelites to "praise the Lord with the musical instruments I have provided for that purpose."[2] In the following book, Hezekiah arranges what must have been a spectacular audiovisual extravaganza.

> He stationed the Levites in the temple of the Lord with cymbals, harps and lyres in the way prescribed by David and Gad the king's seer and Nathan the prophet; this was commanded by the Lord through his prophets. So the Levites stood ready with David's instruments, and the priests with their trumpets. Hezekiah gave the order to sacrifice the burnt offering on the altar. As the offering began, singing to the Lord began also, accompanied by trumpets and the instruments of David king of Israel. The whole assembly bowed in worship, while the musicians played and the trumpets sounded. All this continued until the sacrifice of the burnt offering was completed. (2 Chronicles 29v25-28)

And then there's the actual process of the sacrifices themselves, which, here in 2 Chronicles, involved slaughtering bulls, rams, lambs, and goats, and then splashing the dead animal's blood on an altar.[3] Seems strange—even barbaric—to us, but for Israel, animal sacrifice was imbued with profound symbolism. In animal sacrifice, both the consequences of sin and God's merciful nature were depicted with visceral images and practices. Israel understood themselves as complicit in the corrupting of God's good world, but rather than removing human beings from the picture, God allowed an animal to die in their place. The blood of the animal—which represented life—was sprinkled as a symbolic gesture of God purifying evil. Interestingly, death—even the death of an animal—was not endemic to God's good design for the world. In the Bible, death is God's enemy. And yet, very early in the story of the Bible, we are introduced to animal sacrifice—alien to us, yet ordinary to the world of the ancient Near East. There's never any indication in the text that the blood of a slaughtered animal literally cleansed the defiling effects of evil, but the symbolism invested in the practice communicated something incredible and profoundly true. It did so with violent and upsetting imagery. With splattered blood and blaring trumpets.

JESUS AND CANNABALISM

The same provocative flair is evident in Jesus of Nazareth, who famously preferred parable and metaphor over a consistently literal approach to teaching. That's what an artist does. They utilize their God-given creativity to craft powerfully communicative words, sounds, and visuals that stir the hearts and minds of their audience. When Jesus could have plainly explained the beautiful concept of the Lord's Supper, he goes on a spectacularly grotesque and frustratingly opaque rant about cannibalism. "Very truly I tell you, unless you eat the flesh of the Son of Man and drink his blood, you have no life in you."[4] Jesus says this at a synagogue in Capernaum. To a crowd of people. Some of them say, "How can this man give us his flesh to eat?" Others respond with a simple and hilarious, "This is a hard teaching. Who can accept it?"[5] Jesus is communicating something beautiful, shrouded in the confusing secrecy of a gruesome metaphor. The author even points out that, to the disciples who stuck around, Jesus asks, "Does this offend you?"[6] No explanation. No insider commentary. He asks them plainly. "You do not want to leave too, do you?"[7]

In his magnum opus—his manifesto for discipleship and the kingdom of God, Jesus uses the same measure of gory metaphor. "If your right eye causes you to sin, tear it out and throw it away... And if your right hand causes you to sin, cut it off and throw it away. For it is better that you lose one of your members than that your whole body go into hell."[8]

Jesus' audience—even his own apprentices—often struggled to decode his parables, going so far as to ask why he insisted on using them at all.[9] Some of Jesus's parables are touching stories about discovering treasure,[10] or an estranged son restored to his loving father.[11] Others end with their characters being dismembered.[12] Though Jesus encourages his audience to pay close attention

("Very truly I tell you"), to seek out the meaning in the metaphor ("Whoever has ears, let them hear"), he also admits that his parables are not designed for easy answers nor catered to a wide audience. They're confusing on purpose.

> "This is why I speak to them in parables, Jesus says. 'Though seeing, they do not see; though hearing, they do not hear or understand.'" (Matthew 13v13)

Both Matthew and Mark's biographies of Jesus record a strange incident in which Jesus curses a fruitless fig tree even though it wasn't the season for figs and thus, not really the tree's fault. It is the only recorded *punitive* miracle of Jesus. The act is understood by Bible scholars to be an entirely symbolic gesture intended to demonstrate Jesus' frustration with the "fruitlessness" of Israel. But why? Why did Jesus choose to destroy a plant to make a point? Couldn't he have just described what was on his mind? Because Jesus loves symbolism, even when it takes on a darker tone.

Jesus, a Jewish rabbi, grew up steeped in the Hebrew Scriptures and in a Hebrew understanding of God. The fruit of the fig tree as a symbol of Israel's faithfulness runs throughout the Hebrew Scriptures.[13] Why does Jesus love symbolism? Why would he draw from the rich library of the Hebrew Scriptures, from his imagination, and choose a symbolic gesture rather than a literal one?

Why favor fictional anecdotes when plain exposition may have been less divisive? Less confusing? Why purposefully color some of those narratives with ugly, upsetting metaphors and violent imagery, knowing it could distract from the message?

Because Jesus is an artist.

THE BIBLE AS ART

For centuries of the Christian movement, Jesus's followers have understood the Bible as a library of writings with many human authors and one divine author. The writings of Scripture were "breathed out" by God's Spirit and are thus what God has to say. But God chose the vehicle of human authors without bypassing their unique voices, ideas, and agendas. In that sense, the writings are also what Paul wants to say. Or Nehemiah. Or James. Or Isaiah. Thing is, if God had wanted to inscribe the Bible's content himself and simply hand it to us, conveniently sidestepping any human involvement, he could have done that. In fact, he did once.[14] But God prefers collaboration. In the same way that God selects skilled artists in designing the Tabernacle, directs them with specificity while allowing for creative freedom, God chooses human authors and inspires them. From this counterintuitive collaboration, the human authors wrote what they wanted to write, and the Christian tradition has always recognized that the resultant work is what *God* wanted to say. The implications of this paradox are massive, but for our purposes, notice this: God did not unilaterally control the authoring of the Bible. God was interested in incorporating the artistry of human authors. God wanted to incorporate the artistry of human authors because he wanted the Bible to be a work of art. God is an artist.

There are all kinds of harmful detriment in emphasizing one aspect of the Bible's construction at the expense of the other. Embracing a progressive emphasis on the human authorship at the expense of the divine erodes orthodoxy and eventually dismantles everything fundamental to following Jesus. On the other hand, *de*emphasizing the very *human* element of the Bible's authorship creates all kinds of embarrassing and unnecessary battles over the Bible's ostensibly scientific claims or alleged failure to adhere to modern criteria for recording history. In many cases, this kind of rigid fundamentalism also leads to a falling out with the Bible.

I believe both misunderstandings share a common failure to understand God as an artist. The more theologically liberal view allows for the creativity and quirks of human authors—they see it in the text—but they can't imagine a perfect and divine author interested in and allowing for the subtle and the strange and the abstract. The more theologically conservative view can't imagine a God who would communicate something as crucial as divine truth through artistic means, so they force the entire volume to become an entirely literal and linear one-size-fits-all moral encyclopedia, a manual for life in the modern world—something the Bible does not intend to be. Both views fail to understand God as an artist and the Bible as a work of art. The primary vehicle through which God chooses to speak to his people throughout history is art. After all, the Bible intends to *form* the reader by offering an alternative story. What better way to do that than with art?

To truly appreciate the artistic accomplishment and significance of the Bible requires the spiritual discipline of art appreciation. To appreciate the Bible is to appreciate literature, poetry, discourse, surrealism, symbolism—even the offensive and obscene. That doesn't mean the Bible is fictitious or untrue, but that it is a work of art.

C.S. Lewis talked about the way literature expands the world of the reader. "Those of us who have been true readers all our life seldom fully realise the enormous extension of our being which we owe to authors," he wrote. "We realise it best when we talk with an unliterary friend. He may be full of goodness and good sense but he inhabits a tiny world. In it, we should be suffocated. The man who is contented to be only himself, and therefore less a self, is in prison. My own eyes are not enough for me, I will see through those of others. Reality, even seen through the eyes of many, is not enough. I will see what others have invented…. In reading great literature I become a thousand men and yet remain myself. Like the night sky in the Greek poem, I see with a myriad eyes, but it is still I who see. Here, as in worship, in love, in moral action, and in knowing, I transcend myself; and am never more myself than when I do."[15]

The Bible is unique in the world of literature. It's not really a *book* at all, but a library of writings. The Old Testament alone was drafted over a period of more than a thousand years, and the New Testament a few decades. This library of writings spanning centuries of language and culture combines narrative, poetry, parables, and teaching that coalesces into a single epic volume to tell one story. The Bible has no literary equivalents in terms of form and scope. If I had to make an analogy, I would use Frank Herbert's *Dune*. In some ways, *Dune* is a traditional science fiction novel, but its legacy has to do with the rich and layered universe it creates. Herbert drafted *Dune* after years of extensive ecological research, and the book's primary narrative is set against a complex backdrop that spans millennia. Each chapter is prefaced with quotations from in-universe writings from long after the events of the book. The novel is bookended by appendices and an intergalactic glossary that enriches and expands the story. Herbert was interested in more than space aliens and robots, and he threads *Dune* together with philosophy, religion, and politics. Characters in *Dune* often quote poetry, recite liturgy, reference history, and tell stories within stories, none of which belong to our world but to the world of *Dune*.

Though *Dune* is intended to be read as a single epic volume, it combines numerous genres and forms, references works within and outside of itself, spanning cultures, locations, languages, and millennia. *Dune* is a complicated work of art, but it pales in comparison to the scope of the Bible. Even the literary construction of the Bible itself is a feat of sophisticated artistry. The Biblical authors draw from an extensive toolbox, using everything from poems and song lyrics, symbolic names, images, and number values, history, discourse, and allegory. There's even an entire genre of literature ("Apocalyptic") for which we have no modern equivalent. This lost genre deals almost entirely in over-the-top, highly symbolic images to grapple with suffering, evil, and the hope of salvation.

The Bible has a book called Job that is uniquely set beyond the world of Israel and populated by non-Israelite characters. The book has no historical setting to speak of. Job begins with a prologue, launches into dense Hebrew poetry and dialogue, then closes with an epilogue. Some scholars believe Job may have been something like a play.

Some scholars argue that the book of Jonah—that one where the guy gets swallowed by "a great fish"— is a work of satire.

The Bible boasts an entire book of Hebrew love poetry called The Song of Songs, filled with explicit descriptions of romance and sexual desire. One Puritan commentator once wrote of Song of

Songs, "The Jewish doctors advised their young people not to read it till they were thirty years old."[16] The book is so interestingly open-ended that it has inspired ongoing debate as to why it's in the Bible at all. Today, most scholars believe The Song of Songs stands in a long tradition of ancient romance poetry designed to reflect on and celebrate God's gift of sexual love. Like lyrics to a moving ballad, the book isn't meant to be dismantled and dissected, stripped for academic parts, but simply read as a unified work, and enjoyed. While enjoying Song of Songs, one can't help but notice detailed passages about admiring and desiring a lover's breasts and what sure sound like fruit-based metaphors for oral sex.

These are just a handful of examples of the many styles and forms of literary content a reader uncovers when they open the Bible. There are lots of different genres of writing, but most of the Bible is narrative. From cover to cover, the Bible tells a single story. It's about God creating a good world and people to live there with him. About how the people mess things up and how God enacts a plan to restore the fractured relationship between him and his beloved and to restore a world broken by sin.

This story has endured for millennia as perhaps the most read, debated, dissected, discussed, loved, and hated artifacts of writing in all of human history—religious or otherwise. At some point, you begin to wonder: If the Bible is God's way of telling the story of the universe, of inviting readers into that story, why is it so dense, layered, and complicated? To be fair, the Bible is often clear and exceedingly beautiful, but there are passages that are confounding, bizarre, and deeply upsetting. There are times when the Bible's ugliness serves a clear purpose to the modern reader but not to the characters in the story. Other times, it seems like the characters in the story know exactly what's going on, but the reader has no clue.

There are entire passages and songs in the Bible that dive headlong into suffering, despair, and nihilism. The opening lines of Ecclesiastes read, "Meaningless! Meaningless! Utterly meaningless! Everything is meaningless." David opens Psalm 13— a song intended for a choir—with the lyrics, "How long, O Lord? Will you forget me forever? How long will you hide your face from me? How long must I take counsel in my soul and have sorrow in my heart all the day?"

Sing *that* at church.

Some of these unhappy songs and meditations are resolved on a hopeful note; others kind of hang in the air, as sorrow often does. The Psalms are intended as *meditation literature*. The reader is meant to move slowly, pouring over each word, exercising their imagination to realize the book's vivid imagery. Look at this section of Psalm 137:

Remember, LORD, what the Edomites did on the day Jerusalem fell. "Tear it down," they cried, "tear it down to its foundations!" Daughter Babylon, doomed to destruction, happy is the one who repays you according to what you have done to us. Happy is the one who seizes your infants and dashes them against the rocks.

What kind of visuals do those last lines bring to your mind's eye? And here's the twist: disciples of Jesus are not meant to invoke these prayers today. In fact, we're forbidden from doing so.[17] Why is this in the Bible? These aren't *good* or *uplifting* feelings. We're not meant to emulate them, per se, and the imagery is more extreme than most horror movies. And yet, there it is. Even the history of the Bible is unflinching and graphic. In 2 Kings, a couple of bears maul and mangle 42 children. In Judges 19, a concubine is gang-raped to death before her body is cut into pieces. Her hacked-up remains are then mailed throughout Israel.

There's also graphic language. In Philippians, Paul confesses that everything he once imagined to his credit as a religious leader he now understands to be σκύβαλον (skubalon) compared to the unsurpassable value of knowing Jesus and being known by him. That Greek word "skubalon" is often translated as "garbage" or "rubbish," but it literally means excrement. Some scholars argue it may have been comparable to our English words "crap" or even "shit."

2 Samuel 20v30 documents Saul screaming at Jonathan what is often translated as, "You son of a perverse, rebellious woman!" But the New Living Translation renders the insult, "You stupid son of a whore!" The Message: "You son of a slut!" A footnote in the NET Bible explains: "A better approximation of the sentiments expressed here by the Hebrew phrase would be 'you stupid son of a bitch!'"

I don't talk this way but I read it in my Bible.

Intense language, violence, sex poems, adultery, betrayal, deception, incest, nihilism, orgies, dismemberment, rape, genocide, war, murder, hope and hopelessness. Some of it literal, some of it figurative. Some of it redemptive, some of it somber and bleak. Some of the crazy stuff is in there to teach something, some to record history. Some of it continues to defy easy explanation.

Most of the Bible we understand. On a small handful of passages, there is virtually no consensus amongst scholars or laypeople. This seems to reinforce the idea that God was more interested in the artistic literary design of the Bible on a macro and micro level than he was concerned with every bit of it being palatable and quickly or conveniently understood. Though human authors wrote the Bible, the historic tradition of Christianity has uniformly agreed that it was "breathed out" and "inspired" by God himself. So, the Bible is the way God wanted it to be. Christians commit to receive as truth all that the Bible teaches as the delegated authority of God. And it's a work of art. The Bible itself is a beautiful, complex, confusing, and offensive work of art. It's *more* than that as well, but not less. This is how God tells his story.

THE ART OF GOD

Throughout the Bible, God communicates and interacts with humanity through creative artistry. Through vivid and emblematic visions, parables, and stories. Through pieces and performances that he commissions and commands. He could do it some other way, but he doesn't. God invites his people into deeply symbolic traditions that express and remind us of profound truths. In the Old Testament, it was the sacrificial system, the Passover celebration. Today, it's baptism, the Lord's Supper. These are, in essence, mini-dramas that symbolize a bigger story. Why would God favor symbolism and drama over straightforward, candid clarity? Why does he command tiny theater rather than something more explicit? Less esoteric? Why does God tell Ezekiel to "set forth an allegory and tell it to the Israelites as a parable,"[18] rather than commanding something less vulnerable to misinterpretation? It makes perfect sense: God is an artist.

He is concerned not only for communicative clarity—sometimes, he seems completely uninterested in it. And that's because God doesn't want to simply explain things to you. He wants to know you and for you to know him. What he is like, how he talks, and why. He wants to speak truth to you at the deepest level of your soul. Artists are like that. They want to communicate. They want to be known. We all do. So does God, in whose image we are created.

In Acts 10, the apostle Peter experiences a strange vision. "He saw heaven opened and something like a large sheet being let down to earth by its four corners. It contained all kinds of four-footed animals, as well as reptiles and birds" (v11-12). Shortly thereafter, through unfolding circumstances, Peter understands the vision was a radical declaration of God's intention to spread the message of Jesus beyond the Jewish people. Why not just tell Peter to do that? Why not make it abundantly obvious? Why weird visions of blankets full of owls and alligators? In the vision, a disembodied voice tells Peter to kill the animals in the sheet and eat them; although the sheet is populated entirely by animals the Torah forbade Jewish people from eating. The whole scene is strange and surreal, offensive to Jewish sensibilities, and kind of gross. If you follow the visual, you might imagine Peter storming the white sheet, blood spraying from screeching animals, staining his hands and face. It could have easily been communicated another way, but it wasn't. And it makes perfect sense why: God is an artist. God is the first and best artist and therefore, the most excellent example of what an artist really is. In fact, Paul argues in Romans that one of the primary ways the nature of God is evidenced is through his artwork.

> For since the creation of the world God's invisible qualities—his eternal power and divine nature—have been clearly seen, being understood from what has been made, so that people are without excuse. (Romans 1v20)

The word "people" in the text is the Greek word anthrōpos. Here, it means what you'd guess: humanity. All people. Who can understand God through his artwork? All people. Ordinarily, this verse is wielded as an apologetic from creation. God made the world and we experience it; and thus, the world itself is an argument for God's power, nature, and existence. This is true, but there's more to it than that. This is an apologetic from art.

A few verses prior, Paul mentions the type of people to whom his warning is addressed are the "godless" and "wicked." With his trademark straightforwardness, Paul writes: "What may be known about God is plain to them, because God has made it plain to them" (v18-19). *All* people can know God through his art—even people far from God. Through his art, God can be "made plain" to them. Imagine: A woman weeps before the *Mona Lisa*, lamenting that she can never know Leonardo da Vinci. A bystander smiles. "But you can," they say. "You can know him through his art." If God is—in some meaningful sense—*knowable* through his artwork, and if we are not unlike God in our appointment and ability to create art, then we are similarly knowable through our art. This knowing is not exhaustive (we need special revelation through the Scriptures), but it is meaningful and profound.

However nuanced and complex, Stanley Kubrick can be known, in a certain sense, through his films. Sylva Plath and Emily Dickinson are in their poetry. The self-portraits of Frida Kahlo are more than mere oil and canvas. David Bowie is, in a way, Ziggy Stardust. Marina Abramović was made plain in the six hours of *Rhythm 0*. Stephen King wrote: "I think you will find that, if you continue to write fiction, every character you create is partly you."[19]

When God creates art, it is often an extension of his beautiful nature and, thus, overtly beautiful. But throughout the story of the Bible, God commissions and utilizes art that is also ugly, offensive, and "unnecessarily" complicated. Throughout history, human artists have followed God's example by creating art that is beautiful or ugly, undisguised, or shrouded in metaphor, uplifting or distasteful. The work of beholding and appreciating art is the work of humanity. Sometimes, people understand what art is saying and are affected by it. Sometimes they don't.

Both are okay.

ACT II:
WHAT
IS ART
FOR?

INTERMISSION

THE COILED MILLIPEDE

I USED MY FINGERNAILS to peel back the cellophane wrap, the familiar factory tang of plastic wafting up from the CD's packaging. I slid the cardboard sleeve away from the jewel case and split the clamshell casing. The silver disc glistened inside. On its surface, white ink spiraled in a strange, bone-like pattern. A ram's horn, maybe. A seashell. Possibly a trilobite.

I pinched either side of the disc, careful not to smudge it with oily fingerprints, and set it inside my stereo, drawing the headphones over my ears. This wasn't a record I could play loud. It was a secret. The disc began spinning, a high, thin whirring sound within the black machinations of the stereo and the sounds of the opening track issued from the headphones and into the ears God designed for hearing.

For more than an hour, I sat there, transfixed. The CD's booklet in hand, reading along with the lyrics, puzzling over the strange visuals, and I was changed. My idea of what music was and could be didn't just evolve; it metamorphosed. This thing—this illicit material, purchased and played in secret—had fundamentally reoriented my perspective on art across 14 tracks. And no one could know about it. In my world, no one would understand.

Inside the stereo, the disc went on spinning, a coiled millipede printed on its surface.

CHAPTER 2:1

USEFUL / USELESS / BOTH

On an afternoon in the summer of 1997, Ira Silverberg visited the home of William S. Burroughs. Sometimes referred to as The High Priest of Junk or The Godfather of Punk, Burroughs made a career of the outrageous and bizarre in his writing and visual art. Ira Silverberg had been tasked with editing a single-volume collection of Burroughs's work that best captured his distinct literary voice.

Silverberg delivered the edited manuscript to Burroughs' home a week before Burroughs died. Burroughs nodded at the ten-pound box that contained the completed tome—a sprawling collage of memoir, violence, obscenity, and dreamlike drug-fueled prose. He said, "I think we shall call it *Just for Jolly*. You realize, of course, these are words of Jack the Ripper, uttered in response to a query as to the motivation for his crimes. 'Just for jolly,' he said. And indeed what else shall we call a life's work?"[1] Burroughs was and is a divisive figure in art and literature. Why'd he do it? Why provoke and offend and inspire? Just for jolly.

Art usually does something. It elicits an emotional and/or intellectual response, inspires, provokes, encourages, comforts, rattles, and frustrates us. Entire lives have been changed in the two-hour runtime of a feature film, the forty-five minutes of an album, the moment someone laid eyes on a painting or a photograph, beheld a speech, a performance, a ballet. But does art have to do anything to justify its existence? Is it somehow less valuable than some other utilitarian work if it doesn't?

Filmmaker and puppeteer Frank Oz worked with Jim Henson for years, famously giving life to characters like Grover, Miss Piggie, and Yoda. He recalled a formative moment on the set of Sesame Street in the early 70s. "We're rehearsing a 'Rapunzel' sketch. Jon Stone directing. We're screwing around. Tears in our eyes from laughing. I shout to Jon, 'What are we teaching?' Jon shouts back, 'Who cares!' And he was right. Sometimes just having fun has value all its own."[2]

Who cares?

Francis Schaeffer wrote, "A work of art has a value in itself. For some this principle may seem too obvious to mention, but for many Christians it is unthinkable. And yet if we miss this point, we miss the very essence of art. Art is not something we merely analyze or value for its intellectual content. It is something to be enjoyed." He goes on to offer this advice: "How should an artist begin to do his work as an artist? I would insist that he begin his work as an artist by setting out to make a work of art."[3] That's it.

ART NEEDS NO JUSTIFICATION

An artist does not create motivated by the need to justify their art—front-loading it with extraneous validity. An artist creates to create. Imagine some scrupulous cynic interrogating God for some pragmatic purpose to all creation. Why leopard slugs? Why Brachiosaurs? Why moons and stars? Why poetry? Why visions of shellfish and lizards? Why food cooked over poop? Why blue pomegranates? Why "eat my flesh and drink my blood"? Why not?

Art may be conceived with all manner of profound meaning and purpose, or it might become infused with either along the way or after the fact. Or the creative endeavor begins and ends as a purpose unto itself. Art, in the story of the Bible, is inherently valuable. This truth is evidenced in the way God favors wild artistic expression when plain, unornamented communication would be sufficient, if not preferable. Meaning, in the Bible, God often prefers to communicate via art for no efficient or practical reason to speak of. When we learn to appreciate and admire this—whether we are creative or not—it becomes worship.

Creativity itself is inherently valuable, as it reflects the personhood of the Creator. Part of what it means to be made in God's image is to be creative but to also value and appreciate the creativity of both

God and people made in his image. Art, for art's sake. Not unlike the Tabernacle of Exodus, the Temple described in 2 Chronicles is a feat of thoughtful ornamentation, but not every decoration acts as a symbol. The precious stones placed by Solomon, we read, are there simply to be beautiful.[44] "There was no pragmatic reason for the precious stones," observed Francis Schaeffer. "They had no utilitarian purpose. God simply wanted beauty in the temple. God is interested in beauty."[4]

The text describes freestanding columns festooned with chains and bronze fruit. Again, "they were there only because God said they should be there as a thing of beauty… art work upon art work."[5] There are also representations of angels, flowers, oxen, and lions in this place of worship. Why all this fuss? Does God *need* a lion statue in the temple? Blue pomegranates on a priest's robe? Of course not. He *wants* them there. Could God have conceived a natural order without lunar cycles, waterfalls, giraffes, and iridescent seashells? Sure. But God is not a utilitarian; he is an artist. An artist creates art. Could God have warned Israel of impending danger without flaming feces? Obviously. Could Jesus have warned of the destructive effects of lust without visual metaphors of self-mutilation? Sure. But art communicates to the heart, the mind, and the soul. Shock, offense, and symbolism are often more effective than instruction manuals.

The story of the Bible opens with God as an artist. In a single line, the author of Genesis collapses everything from snow-capped mountain ranges to platypuses into the creative mastermind of the one true God. This essence of creativity is one important dimension of what it means to be made in God's image. To worship God includes acknowledgment and admiration of his artistic sensibility and craftsmanship and the creativity he imbues in human artists. Some art serves a practical purpose; much of it exists simply because it is awesome. Not everyone can be "creative" as per the common understanding of the word, but everyone can honor and reverence creativity as an attribute of God, observed in creation and exemplified by people.

For disciples of Jesus, the spiritual discipline of art appreciation is not optional.

CHAPTER 2:2

MUSEUM WITH NO EXITS

NEW YORK, 1964: ANDY Warhol exhibits stacks of plywood boxes, hand-stenciled to perfectly replicate Brillo brand soap pad packaging. There was no visible difference between Warhol's gallery pieces and the consumer cartons of Brillo pads found in any given supermarket display. Philosopher and art critic Arthur Danto was both fascinated and conflicted by the gallery, writing, "Is… the whole world consisting of latent artworks waiting, like the bread and wine of reality, to be transfigured, through some dark mystery, into the indiscernible flesh and blood of the sacrament? Never mind that the Brillo box may not be good, much less great art. The impressive thing is that it is art at all. But if it is, why are not the indiscernible Brillo boxes that are in the stockroom. Or has the whole distinction between art and reality broken down?"[1] Danto's meditation was concerned with identifying a distinction between what is art and what is not art.

In the end, the distinction is often ambiguous at best. It's unlikely that the corporate powers-that-be at Brillo were preoccupied with pure artistry when commissioning the design of the boxes Warhol would later replicate—but *someone* designed them. And they did so artistically. Warhol's recontextualizing of these consumer artifacts draws our attention to this overlooked artistry. His placing them in an art gallery adds commentary to it.

BALLET DANCERS &
PROFESSIONAL WRESTLERS

Director Darron Aronofsky followed his fourth film, *The Wrestler*, with the ballet body horror freakout *Black Swan*. The former is the tragedy of a professional wrestling has-been, the latter is about an aspiring dancer in a prominent New York company. "I've always considered the two films companion pieces," Aronofsky said. "They are really connected and people will see the connections. It's funny, because wrestling some consider the lowest art — if they would even call it art — and ballet some people consider the highest art. But what was amazing to me was how similar the performers in both of these worlds are. They both make incredible use of their bodies to express themselves."[2]

The performance art of movement, theatrics, and bodily discipline is on full display in ballet and professional wrestling: "High" art and "low" art. Art permeates every culture, social sphere, and all of waking life. It's everywhere. All the time. Whether you go looking for it in *Swan Lake*, snicker at the sparkly spandex of a wrestler on the turnbuckle or pass a soapbox in the storeroom—

art is everywhere.

Thoughtful art appreciation is often assumed to belong to a minority of enthusiasts and experts. Many suspect the nuance and intricacies of creativity are things best understood by those who are themselves creative or who have the particular wiring and palette for such expertise, but the Bible doesn't make either distinction. While it's true that art appreciation, like any discipline or field, can be honed and enriched with education and experience, it's also true that anyone can appreciate art. The rich and the poor, the righteous and unrighteous, the simple and the learned are all equally invited into the spectacle of art created by God and by people. Imagine an unmoved Israelite snorting their disapproval at Hezekiah's musicians as they soundtracked the heavy atmosphere of the burned offering, saying, "So pretentious." Imagine someone shrugging off David's 4,000-person orchestra as "artsy-fartsy." Imagine Ezekiel sneering at God's glorious appearance in humanoid animal creatures and a blazing altar throne, "I don't get it."

Imagine the crowds leaving Jesus' teaching. "He doesn't have to be so gross with all that flesh-eating nonsense." What if Peter had not taken up the mission to the Gentiles because he "isn't the creative type" and didn't bother interpreting or appreciating the imagery of his divine vision? The world and existence are God's art museum, and there's no way out. While some imagine themselves less inclined to the art world than others, we all engage and exploit art every day. In his book *Art for God's Sake*, Philip Graham Ryken notes that "even Christians who are dismissive of art continue to use it."[3]

THE STARTLING SECRET BEHIND ART: ARTISTS

It's easy to dehumanize art, but it isn't right. We tend to reduce art to consumable goods. We segregate art into "high" and "low," "profound" or "popcorn," "worthwhile" or "waste of time." Martin Scorsese thinks superhero movies "aren't cinema."[4] Whatever. Though there is often a consumer element to art and entertainment, there is just as often an unseen dimension of real significance in everything from billboards to pop songs for those prepared to see it. Behind every human-made work of art, there are, you guessed it, people. Even a replicated and repurposed carton of soap pads is worth further investigation.

British filmmaker Alan Parker once said, "No one sets out to make a bad movie."[5] He's right. Creating a feature film requires the ongoing efforts of dozens, even hundreds of individuals. This is true of Oscar-bait prestige pictures just as it is true of effects-driven summer blockbusters and schlocky slasher flicks. Many viewers consume these films in their 90-minute runtime, pass immediate judgment on them—"good" or "bad"—and move on to the next thing. We think of movies, songs, and television shows as soulless content bytes presented for our satisfaction or condemnation. But even when there are record labels, studios, and corporations fronting the bill, behind the shots, songs, and visual effects are real people who usually set out to make something good. Someone drew storyboards and designed costumes. Someone supervised the script and drove actors to locations. Sure, there are movies and songs conceived as little more than cash grabs, but someone still *created* something. Even though a studio wrote checks and issued memos, maybe a director worked hard. Even though a manager and a producer may have curated the image and sound of a pop princess, someone wrote songs, played instruments, sang.

In an effort to clear compounding debt and care for his aging mother, Nicholas Cage spent a decade acting in four movies a year to scare up the necessary cash. Cage said of this desperate sting of roles, "I still had to find something in them to be able to give it my all… Some of them didn't work. But I never phoned it in. So if there was a misconception, it was that. That I was just doing it and not caring. I *was* caring."[6] Even in the terrible overlap of art and commerce, someone usually cares. Someone tried.

Of course, not all art is equally thoughtful or authentic or even good. It isn't. But art is everywhere. Every day, you are likely bombarded with any number of things someone created as an outworking of their artistic ability. Some of it may be profound and soul-stirring, some of it lousy and immoral, but it's everywhere.

You—whether you're an artist or not—make creative decisions every day. Almost every human chooses to interact with objects based on their *aesthetic* value rather than their *functional* value on a regular basis. You are making creative decisions whenever you get dressed, furnish your home, choose one color instead of another, listen to music, or watch a movie or TV miniseries. Every time you pass a billboard or even lift a box of soap in a grocery store aisle, you are privy to the creativity of people, for better or for worse.

The creativity of people reflects the creativity of God, which is similarly inescapable in the ordinary rhythm of life. When you see a tree or a ladybug, a crow, or a kitten, when you admire the unique personalities of your children or spouse or friends, when you behold a sunrise or a mountain range, you are witnessing the creativity of God. All of life is an art museum without exits. The high art elitist cannot avoid daily exposure to "low" art. The art skeptics who imagine themselves creatively ignorant cannot escape a world overflowing with the beauty and ugliness of art. This is a good thing. More than that, it is an invitation to develop the spiritual discipline of art appreciation. After all, if art was God's idea, if he imbues his image-bearers with creative prowess, and if we populate God's world with creativity, ought not all people work to find something in it to reverence?

If so, how do we do that correctly?

ACT III:
WHAT
DO WE
DO
WITH
ART?

INTERMISSION

SIN IN THE CAMP

IN THE SEVENTH CHAPTER of Joshua, a man called Achan steals certain things meant to be dedicated to God, and he lies about it. Eventually, Israel discovers this heinous thing Achan has done, and they confront him. It's true, he tells them. I did it. There was sin in the camp. That's the story our youth pastor told a group of my friends when they asked him what to do about the record I'd bought. Once spinning secretly in my stereo, I couldn't keep the album hidden forever—so great was its impact on me. Sharing my enthusiasm, it turned out, was a mistake.

"There's sin in the camp," my youth pastor told my friends. "What are you doing to do about it?"

So, a group of them went into my room, found the offending disc, and shattered it to pieces. The image of the coiled millipede gleamed up from jagged plastic fragments on the floor.

CHAPTER 3:1

THE DEATH OF CHRISTIAN ART

WHEN DIRECTOR KEVIN SMITH'S film *Dogma* was released in 1999, it attracted a predictable amount of controversy. In it, God (played by Alanis Morrissette) has gone missing after visiting Earth in human form to play Skee-Ball. There's also a demon made of poop, and said demon is one of the least outrageous things in the movie. So, when Kevin Smith learned of Christians protesting the movie in his hometown, he decided to join them. The protestors had no idea the bearded gentleman among them was the film's director. As fate would have it, the local news appeared to cover the protest. Recognizing Smith, they asked for an interview. Smith would not admit his actual identity, remaining in character as an outraged Christian. When asked for his take on *Dogma*, he told reporters, "I don't think it stands for anything positive."

"What *does* it stand for?" they asked.

"I don't know," he said. "But I've been told it's not good."

When Smith later described the strange scene during a Q&A session at Cornell University, he remembered telling the reporters he hadn't seen the movie he was protesting. "Y'know," he told the audience, "because I wanted to be in character." The joke ignited immediate laughter from those in attendance. They all knew that those who object to art most vocally have often made no attempt to understand it. Whether they come armed with picket signs or social media outrage, it's not hard to find droves of furious groups and individuals deeply offended by books they haven't read, albums they haven't heard, and movies they haven't seen or attempted to understand.

Dogma begins with a self-aware disclaimer: "This film is… a work of comedic fantasy, not to be taken seriously. To insist that any of what follows is incendiary or inflammatory is to miss our intention and pass undue judgment; and passing judgment is reserved for God and God alone… Remember: even God has a sense of humor. Just look at the Platypus."[1]

SATANIC PANIC!

Christians collectively devalue art when they divide it into two distinct categories: *Christian* art and *secular* art. The 1980s were marked by a kind of paranoid moral hysteria amongst evangelical Christians. So much so that the period is often described as The Satanic Panic. And it didn't come out of nowhere. The Manson Family murders shocked America in 1969—the same year Anton

LaVey published *The Satanic Bible*. William Peter Blatty's novel *The Exorcist* was released in 1971, and the film adaptation that followed in '73 became a full-fledged pop-culture phenomenon. The devil and his mysterious "occult" were garnering more public attention than ever before. By the time the '70s gave way to the '80s, Christians had begun to see the devil behind every bush—especially in art and entertainment. Evangelical conservatism became hyper-fundamentalism. The fear was this: exposure to and consumption of any art or entertainment not overtly Christian corrupts a person to the degree that their life may become an outworking of the corruption within. So, in Satanic Panic think, if you listen to heavy metal records, you'll be duped into joining the occult by dark imagery and coded messages. If you watch a movie with a sex scene, you'll masturbate or take up a lecherous lifestyle. Hearing swear words makes you say swear words. Fictional violence generates actual violence. Fantasy magic creates Wiccans.

This kind of entertainment legalism mostly died off within a generation. Millennials and Gen-Xers love to trade war stories about our fundamentalist upbringings.

"I wasn't allowed to watch *He-Man and the Masters of the Universe!*"

"Well, *I* wasn't even allowed to watch *The Smurfs!*"

But the Satanic Panic never ended; it evolved. Today's vocal moral watchdogs aren't as likely to wring their hands and clutch their pearls at animated wizards or gangsta rap as they are any language, imagery, or artists that depart from the progressive moral rulebook. At the time of writing, moral panic has graduated from satanic imagery and swear words to representation and identity politics. In the late '90s, hysterical conservatives wanted to host Harry Potter book burnings for fear of their children being led astray by witchcraft. As I write this, hysterical progressives want to host Harry Potter book burnings because author J.K. Rowling refuses to align with a particular gender ideology.

Many disciples of Jesus coming from what we once called an "evangelical" tradition (before the word became entirely political) have adopted a shrugging "whatever" attitude about the art that so worried our parents, or else we simply migrated to the other side of the aisle, embracing that which offended our parents, rejecting all the safe, sanitary Christian art they so loved. Take that, Mom and Dad! Of course, the new progressive art legalism is every bit as problematic as conservative fundamentalism. Neither exhibits a trace of thoughtful theological nuance, Holy Spirit-led discernment, or community-based accountability. Instead, both philosophies are steered by a herd mentality. Everyone is offended? I guess I should be, too. Everyone is suddenly okay with everything? I guess everything is OK. Cultural moral panic over art and entertainment is typically rooted in unthinking mob logic.

Likely reacting to the lackadaisical "anything goes" technique, old-school thinkers conjure up the lingering ghost of the Satanic Panic in an attempt to reanimate its corpse. While Christian discernment bloggers are driven to frenzy by the popularity of *Deadpool* and *Game of Thrones,* progressive journalists throw digital tantrums over a "fatphobic" cartoon dog for saying, "I need some exercise."[2] Go browse the comment section when *Christianity Today* reviews an R-rated film. Waste a few minutes reading about suburban white mom conspiracy theories involving Hollywood, politicians, and devil-worshipping Disney cannibal cults.

The modern leftovers of the Satanic Panic may seem less extreme, but they stand on the same faulty premise. The watered-down (but equally problematic) logic now goes: Depictions of things are always endorsements of things, and beholding and consuming these endorsements makes the consumer complicit in the endorsement and thus corrupts the soul. The weirdest evolution of Satanic Panic logic is its unreasoned and arbitrary selection of offenders. Some pastors may love to quote notoriously crass and sexualized celebrity rappers if they mention Jesus from time to time but draw a hard line at the notoriously crass and sexualized TV miniseries of the moment. At least the fundamentalists of yesteryear were consistent. If He-Man is out, then by God, the Smurfs are out too.

Within fundamentalist logic, art is always objectified. It doesn't matter what *The Exorcist* communicates to an audience. What matters is that there is a demon in it, and demons are bad. It doesn't matter that the Harry Potter series is about friendship, family, good triumphing over evil—what matters is that there are magic spells in it, and magic spells are always bad. Or that the author thinks certain things with which certain readers disagree, and therefore, must be destroyed. The significance of the Venus de Milo is secondary to the fact that her breasts are exposed. Breasts make men lust. Lust is bad. Thus, *The Exorcist*, Harry Potter, and the Venus de Milo are bad! Dangerous! Garbage!

The art moralist is like Frankenstein's monster, waving an outraged arm over any given work of art. Fire *bad*! Fire *bad*! To pull off this level of discriminating moralism requires a fundamental presupposition. If you insist on separating art into broad, black-and-white "good" and "bad" categories, you must concede that art is ultimately expendable. So maybe *The Catcher in the Rye* can move you, make you think, stir your soul, challenge your faith— but it also has swearing, sex, and sacrilege. When in doubt, throw it out. After all, it's just a novel. This logic is a kind of heresy.

In his book *Echoes of Eden*, scholar Jerram Barr writes about this level of dismissiveness, arguing, "In this view, the arts are considered optional, rather extravagant, an unnecessary extra in life. But this belief is nonsense and, according to Paul, a heresy of the most serious kind, for in the end it is a denial of the goodness of creation and the goodness of its Creator."[3] Disciples of Jesus reject the idea that taking pleasure in life on Earth is somehow unspiritual or even sinful. Even the old curmudgeon John Calvin took issue with such an idea, writing, "Should the Lord have attracted our eyes to the beauty of flowers, and our sense of smell to pleasant odors, and should it then be sin to drink them in? Has he not even made the colors so that the one is more wonderful than the other?"[4]

God is the original artist (and occasionally, an ambiguous and offensive one at that). When we assault artwork with a moral measuring stick—whether the measuring stick is conservative or progressive—we do an injustice to our God-given role as those intended to create and appreciate creativity. God himself values artistic expression. God often prefers it. The potential to shock or offend doesn't deter God, or Ezekiel, or Jesus, or the authors of the Bible. They don't shy away from ambiguous surrealism, strong language, violent scenes and metaphors, sexually explicit language and imagery.

When it comes to art, the Church of Jesus enjoys a largely forgotten heritage and a largely *un*forgotten bad reputation. Many monumental figures of the art world also claimed to be Christians—Shakespeare, Rembrandt, Van Gogh, Tolkien, C.S. Lewis, Jane Austen, Andy Warhol, T.S. Eliot, Bach, and on down the list. I have no idea what one might say about the authenticity of their faith, but their stories, thinking, and their work are connected to a

Christian heritage. Even so, today's Christians (especially West-ern Evangelicals) are largely considered artistically illiterate and not without cause. In the '90s, conservative Christians were known for boycotting movies, picketing concerts, smashing CDs, and vandalizing museum exhibits. A couple of decades later, pro-gressive Christians are known for online outrage and cancel cul-ture. They're both sort of the same thing.

SACRED, SANITIZED, & WHOLESOMELY INOFFENSIVE

All too often, many Christians would like to ingest or condemn complex works of creativity with some imaginary, black-and-white rubric of morality they create for themselves. But this mor-alistic measuring stick is invariably subjective. It never works the same from person to person precisely because art is complex in its ability to uplift or offend. When Christians insist on segregating art, the inevitable outgrowth is "Christian" art. Everything that is not explicitly Christian and appropriately sanitized must make way for comrade-approved "clean" art as if some art were sacred, and everything else inevitably relegated to the dreadful secular realm. An effort like this becomes a fool's errand.

Jerram Barr argues, "Even those who suggest most passionately that Christians should only enjoy art by other Christians will take delight in buildings, bridges, roads, interior decoration, clothes, or beautifully prepared and presented meals, and they will take this delight without asking whether the architect, builder, designer, manufacturer, or chef is a committed believer in the Lord Jesus Christ... The truth is that there is not a single Christian in the world who does not daily benefit from the creative gifts and hard work of the unbelievers around him or her."[5]

The sacred/secular divide has more to do with Platonic thinking than with Christian theology. Plato believed in a sharp distinction between spiritual (good) and physical (bad). But this is not the worldview of Jesus nor the authors of the Bible. Author John Mark Comer puts it this way, "Jesus didn't buy into sacred/secular thinking. Not one bit. To him, the God he called Father is as close as the air up against our skin. To him, life is a seamless, integrated, holistic experience where the sacred is all around us."[6]

Eventually, the grassroots movement of Christianity extended beyond Jerusalem and into the Greco-Roman world—to Athens, the home of Plato. Centuries later, the influence of Greek thinking is evident in the modern Christian understanding of some things as "spiritual" and other things as "not spiritual." Thus, for many Christians, going to church is spiritual. Eating a sandwich is not. Praying is spiritual. Talking to a friend about the weather is not. Songs written for the clear and express purpose of worshipping God are spiritual. Songs about existential dread or sexual frustration are not. If this is true, then Christians have little choice but to create "Christian" art if they're going to enjoy any art at all.

Christian songs, Christian movies, Christian paintings. Here, "Christian" means "overt and obvious, purged of anything secular." If it isn't *obviously* Christian, it isn't Christian at all. Philip Graham Ryken argues, "Some Christians continue to think that certain forms of art are more godly than others. They make a sharp distinction between the sacred and the secular, not recognizing that so-called secular art is an exploration of the world that God has made, and therefore has its place in deepening our understanding of God's person and work."[7]

One of the many problems with this heresy of sacred vs. secular is that it inevitably spills over into the landscape of all vocation and enjoyment. If the "Christian art" standard is to be upheld, all "secular" vocations and outlets for enjoyment must be abandoned for more overtly Christianized ones. Teachers, engineers, mechanics, baristas, plumbers, accountants, administrators, and everyone in between should flee their secular fields and apply at churches and non-profits (but only Christian ones). How ridiculous.

C.S. Lewis argued, "The rules for writing a good passion play or a good devotional lyric are simply the rules for writing tragedy or lyric in general."[8] Disciples of Jesus are invited by their master to excel in their unique God-given vocations and callings, not to Christianize and segregate them according to evolving sensibilities. Writer Flannery O'Connor remains one of the great figures of literature, and she wrote novels and stories that dealt openly with her faith. But O'Connor's stories are also famously upsetting and grotesque, and her work has been celebrated and emulated for decades by readers and writers, both Christian and otherwise. Readers recognize in O'Connor's writing a stark sincerity. Flannery O'Connor is not pigeonholed as a "Christian writer," she is recognized the world over as a great author. Bishop Robert Barron said of Flannery O'Connor, "She gave glory to God primarily in the act of fashioning a story *well*. So, people would say to her, 'If you're Catholic and you want to write on Catholic themes, why aren't you writing about priests and nuns and monasteries?' And she would say, 'Well, you could, but a properly crafted story… That will give glory to God in itself.'"[9]

In other words, want to make "Christian" art? Just make good art.

THE PEOPLE VS. AMY GRANT

In the late 70s, Amy Grant became one of the pioneering figures of what was eventually described as "Contemporary Christian Music." By the '80s, Christians were ready to disown her.

"While many evangelicals hailed Ms. Grant as a musical ambassador to mainstream culture, others greeted her professional triumphs with complaints that she was too worldly and too sexy," writes a *New York Times* columnist. "Her energetic performance on the 1985 Grammy Awards telecast offended some evangelicals, who considered her leopard-print jacket and bare feet

improper… A writer in the evangelical magazine Christianity Today criticized Ms. Grant's 1997 release, 'Behind the Eyes,' for its
'complete absence of explicitly Christian lyrical content.' The ensuing controversy prompted the Gospel Music Association to
adopt content requirements for its annual Dove Award entries."[58]
Note the language used against Amy Grant in *Christianity Today*:
"Complete absence of explicitly Christian lyrical content." This
from an article more than two decades old, while many Christians
persist in this same narrow mindset today. When we demand that
art adhere to the "explicitly Christian" rulebook, something inevitable happens: Bad art.

In Donald Ray Pollock's sublime masterwork of Southern Gothic
literature, *The Devil All the Time,* a serial killer named Carl scoffs
at an inoffensive piece of hotel wall art. Carl, who photographs his
victims, believes his pictures of torture and death are more artistically credible than a framed image of fruit because one, while
pleasant enough, is entirely forgettable. The other, though horrifying, is impossible to forget. Carl's photographs are upsetting,
but they are sincere. The Christian intersection of art and commerce cranks out plenty of milquetoast consumables as inoffensive as they are forgettable. If we throw out the formula, things
might get ugly from time to time, but they'll also be a whole heck
of a lot more honest and, dare I say, interesting.

If you think this antiquated '80s aversion to Amy Grant a relic of a time long since passed, then watch what happens when a worship artist deviates from the industry-approved standard dictated by the two or three megachurch bands monopolizing the genre. The objections will be swift and merciless. "It's fine," people may say, "but it isn't worship music." By and large, we still believe Christian art should be obvious. Worship songs must include paint-by-numbers melodies, traditionally sing-songy choruses, culturally Christian buzz words, delay pedals. I've often attempted sharing one song or another that I found particularly excellent for worship and watched as the confused listener screwed up their face in disapproval, saying, "This doesn't *sound* like worship." As if all worship had one distinct sound.

For many, worship songs are not abstract or experimental, never complicated or melancholy, never beyond the norm of industry trends. And they are always explicitly "churchy." Don't get me wrong, it's not that explicitly Christian themes are always bad; it's that explicitly Christian expectations and requirements always cripple artistry. Think about it. If the only safe zone for Christian art is the cultural standard of "explicitly Christian," then most of the human experience is off-limits. Things like romance, sexuality, loneliness, despair, apathy, simple beauty, and delight are all off the table unless they are somehow crowded with readily apparent nods to God and the Bible.

I genuinely enjoy singing songs at church on Sunday, but most of the songs we sing aren't the kinds of songs I would listen to just to enjoy as a piece of music, personally. There are lots of other songs that would probably not be the best fit for Sunday worship, songs that I enjoy aesthetically, and that evoke a deep, visceral responses in me and compel me to worship. That doesn't make the second kind of song better than the first one, but it illustrates the wide and varied spectrum of a given audience. A song that most affects me could show up on an album that is vulgar and macabre, while some of the songs we sing at my church might represent what has become a staple of mainstream worship music. I would never be so bold as to argue that all mainstream worship music is creatively bankrupt, but I do believe that drawing parameters around what qualifies as "Christian art" inevitably bankrupts creativity.

This unforgiving rulebook empties the artist's toolbox. No subtlety, no metaphor, no shock, no thoughtfulness. Spoon-feed the audience. Make plain the intended message. Clear away the ambiguity, comrade! According to these rules, God himself would be denied creative license.

I once wrote a song called "Dear John Piper (Stillbirth in Space)" with decidedly abrasive lyrics. The song is an indictment of a particular theological paradigm with which I have massive, heated disagreement. To no one's surprise, it ruffled a few feathers. What interested me in the hubbub of outrage, Internet comments, and discernment vloggers wasn't that some were in a hurry to defend the theological position I had lampooned. That much was to be expected. What surprised me was the massive ignorance on display as to the role and function of song lyrics. Song lyrics are not theological essays. Thus, they should not be engaged as such. Imagine if, instead of writing this song, I had painted something. Imagine the painting was of famous pastor and author John Piper depicted as Gollum from *The Lord of the Rings*. In his hands, this Gollum-Piper clutches a wilted tulip as he sneers, *"Preciousssss…"*

This painting would act as a thinly veiled metaphorical statement on the way we tend to make idols of theological systems (T.U.L.I.P. being a famous acronym used to explain five tenets of Calvinist theology to which Piper subscribes). Would a painting like this irk a particular audience? Obviously. Maybe they'd argue that the statement made by the painting wasn't fair or accurate, and maybe they'd be right. But what if, amidst the backlash, someone pointed to the painting and cried, "John Piper doesn't look like that! He doesn't carry a dead flower! He doesn't talk like Gollum! This is not a real picture of John Piper!" Well, no, of course not. A surreal or satirical painting is not a "realistic" portrait. Satire isn't literal. It isn't meant to be. Just as theological lyrics to a punk rock song are not an academic essay on systematic theology. Why engage them as such? Of course, that doesn't mean an artist should never take any responsibility for their work, but just as an artist must own that which they create, so the beholder must own their interpretation. That many rigid personalities insisted on interacting with this song I'd written as if it was an essay was funny and all, but it also indicated something more troubling than ordinary and expected theological disagreement: Many disciples of Jesus do not understand essential artistic components like satire, hyperbole, and surrealism. We don't know how to engage art.

Built into the critique of this song was a sinister implication: Art should be emptied of all that is complicated and abstract. As if these outraged listeners were scanning God's plans for the tabernacle in dismay, "Pomegranates are not blue!" The shackling of Christian art confines Christian artists within a bubble designed to hamper them and destroy their creativity. With severely restricted access to the arts, aspiring Christian artists have only severely restricted art from which to draw inspiration. So, they make more severely restricted art, derivative of already-severely-restricted art. A copy of a copy. What else can they do?

My wife and I sometimes play a discouraging game while traveling. As we drive, we scan local radio stations. The game's object is to identify the station playing "Christian" music before the lyrics give it away. In other words, spot the Christian station based solely on how lame the music sounds. We win this game every time. You can play the same game at the movies. Every few years, the Christian industry rallies enough funds to churn out a major motion picture. Sometimes, the movie has enough megachurch budget for wide distribution and garners mainstream press. You might even catch a trailer at your local movie theater. During the opening fifteen seconds of one such trailer in recent memory—before anything overtly Christian had been said or done—my friend leaned over to me and said, "Oh no, this looks Christian." In a *Hollywood Reporter* review of a 2019 "Christian movie," one journalist muses, "One wonders why [the film], which resembles a basic cable television movie in its mediocre production values and subpar performances, was made."[10] Defensive Christians might fire back with accusations of Hollywood bias, but I'm not so sure.

These radio stations, these movie trailers, they often look and sound insincere and inauthentic, like someone playing at real music or real filmmaking. They seem phony somehow. Maybe generic is one way of putting it. Out of touch. Derivative. Products designed by committee to sell something sanitized, something that adheres to an absolute moral standard. Something designed without design in mind—a ruse to gather converts, not an honest effort to create art for art's sake.

Thomas Merton wrote, "A bad book about the love of God remains a bad book, even though it may be about the love of God. There are many who think that because they have written about God, they have written good books. Then men pick up these books and say: if the ones who say they believe in God cannot find anything better than this to say about it, their religion cannot be worth much."[11] Talk to artists and musicians who have contributed to small churches, and most of them will likely have stories about the rampant disregard for aesthetic excellence. When asked why more care was not given to rehearsal, why more thought was not dedicated to aesthetics, why worship bands were haphazardly populated with incapable or underdeveloped musicians, these artists and musicians were often told such concerns were frivolities. That God cared about the heart of the lousy drummer, not about his lousy drumming. That aesthetics amounted to pageantry, a distraction from what *really* matters. This kind of logic dishonors God.

A person's artistic abilities contribute nothing to their inherent value before God, but to suggest that talent (or lack thereof) is inconsequential doesn't just diminish the capabilities of the artist; it belittles the craftsmanship of God himself. From cover to cover, the Bible insists that though all humans are made in God's image and are of equal value, every person is uniquely designed by God with a calling and a purpose. To flatten the uniqueness of our God-given design demonstrates an outrageous disregard for the Scriptures. We tend to think that telling someone, "Hey, maybe drums aren't your thing," is an assault on their dignity, But God doesn't see it that way.

In Exodus 31, when God looks out on all his people—capable and incapable, "good hearts" and buttheads alike—he says, "See, I have chosen Bezalel… and I have filled him with the Spirit of God, with wisdom, with understanding, with knowledge and with all kinds of skills—to make artistic designs."[12] God takes no issue whatsoever with saying, Have this guy do it, not some other guy. If "heart" was all that mattered, God might've asked *Moses* to "make artistic designs" for the Tabernacle. He doesn't. God specifically selects artists over and against all others precisely because God has given them "all kinds of skills." If God invited anyone willing to contribute to make artistic designs for the Tabernacle, I'm sure the whole thing would have been done a lot faster. But several times, God commands Moses that the workers must be creatively qualified.[13]

Despite God's obvious concern for capability, for aesthetics and symbolism, for surrealism and shock value, Christian culture seems to have codified a standard for art that devalues—often condemns—all of these things. Not even the teachings of Jesus always meet the cultural Christian art standard. Theologian Stanley Hauerwas described the parables of Jesus as: "Extended metaphors or comparisons designed to draw the hearer into a new awareness of reality as revealed by Jesus, yet their artful nature adds a special twist of paradox and unexpected challenge."[14] Jesus told ambiguous, veiled, and artful stories when plain teaching would have certainly been the clearer means of communication. Case in point, his followers ask him outright, "Why do you speak to the people in parables?" Drawing from the prophet Isaiah, Jesus explains that his parables are intentionally enigmatic, at least for some people.[15] In the book of Isaiah, the prophet experiences a powerful vision in which God commands that Israel be warned of their coming judgment, even though they are so far gone that they will not listen to Isaiah's message.[16] Jesus's message, like Isaiah's, will have a paradoxical effect on his listeners: The power of stories—even cryptic, metaphorical ones—will penetrate the hearts of some while hardening the hearts of others.

In his commentary on Matthew's gospel, R.T. France describes a parable as "An utterance which does not carry its meaning on the surface, and which thus demands thought and perception if the hearer is to benefit from it. Learning from and responding to a parable is not a matter of simply reading off the meaning from the words, but of entering into an interactive process to which the hearer must contribute if true understanding is to result... The same parable which enlightens one may puzzle or even repel another. A parable is not an easy option for understanding, but a challenge to which not everyone will be able to rise."[17] France is describing the process of interpretation. An artist understands that to craft something for maximum impact, creative decisions must be made that will inevitably alienate some of the audience. But, the groupthink of "Christian art" insists that the artist take creative cues from cultural sensibilities rather than God. The institution that became frustrated with Amy Grant wasn't the Church; it was the Christian Music Industry—an industry concerned with product and profit. Sanitized product sells. Clarity and simplicity sell. Subtlety and metaphor don't always sell. Shocking imagery—regardless of how powerfully it communicates—doesn't always sell. Just ask Jesus.

Jesus: "Eat my flesh. Drink my blood... Does this offend you?"

Audiences: "This is a hard teaching. Who can accept it?"

But for Jesus, it's *all* spiritual. It's *all* theological. The same is true of art. There is no "Christian music" in the theological sense because art itself is inherently Christian. The category of "Christian music" is an industry term, not a theological one. Movies about wizards and aliens are spiritual. Songs about teen angst and dancing are spiritual. Novels about detectives and serial killers are spiritual. Paintings of landscapes and abstract shapes are spiritual. Boxes of soap pads are spiritual. Everything in the human experience—good and bad—is appropriate material for the arts, just as it is appropriate and well represented in the artistry of the Bible.

2 Samuel 13 features a horrible rape scene. It features a horrible person doing a horrible thing. Knowing her brother Amnon is about to force himself on her, Tamar begs him to reconsider. He does not. After Amnon has raped his sister, he has her dragged from the room. Tamar is told by her other brother to keep the incident to herself. The author describes her as "disgraced" and

"desolate." Doesn't this story resonate with the human experience in ways that are direct (for some) and indirect (for others)? The world is broken, often evil. Is a disciple of Jesus not free to examine and sort through this story artistically— to unpack the raw, devastating emotion, ugliness, the "intense hatred" described by the author?[18] Shouldn't there be a place to welcome and experience art of this "ugly" kind—the kind that provides an outlet for us to sort through the broken human experience? Yes. This is crucial.

But are there no limits? Sexuality is spiritual, but sexuality can be corrupted. Violence can be depicted fictionally for profound communicative purposes, but violence is evil. The spirituality of all things does not guarantee of the goodness of all things. An appreciation for the context of depiction and the sophisticated nuance of artistry does not guarantee that all art is suitable for all people.

So, how do you figure *that* one out?

CHAPTER 3:2
CONTEXT! CONVICTION! CONTROVERSY!

WHEN BRET EASTON ELLIS'S novel *American Psycho* was released in 1991, people got upset. Tammy Bruce—then-president of the Los Angeles Chapter of the National Organization for Women—called for a boycott. "This is not art," she said. "Mr. Ellis is a confused, sick young man with a deep hatred of women who will do anything for a fast buck… Ellis could have gone on writing until he choked on his own vomit if Vintage [the publishing house] had not agreed to publish this misogynistic garbage."[19]

American Psycho is narrated by Patrick Bateman, a successful Wall Street yuppie in 1980s New York who describes his wardrobe, workout routine, record collection, and methods of raping and mutilating women, all with the same excessive and exhausting deadpan detail. Outrageous though it may be, *American Pyscho*'s author argued that the novel's passages of extreme violence were not celebratory. He didn't, in other words, *like* the things he was depicting in his novel. "I would think most Americans learn in junior high to differentiate between the writer and the character he is writing about," said Ellis. "People seem to insist I'm a monster. But Bateman is the monster." Author J.M. Sterling put things a bit more frankly, writing, "There is a technical, literary term for those who mistake the opinions and beliefs of characters in a novel for those of the author. That term is 'idiot.'"[20]

Guinevere Turner was one of two women to write the film adaptation of *American Psycho*. She saw something in this story of a mass-murdering socialite other than misogyny. "Bret really thought he was writing a feminist book," she said years later. "I remember seeing him speak and really talk about that and how he was actually hurt and shocked that feminists spoke out against his book because he thought he was writing a feminist book and that's what we saw in it."[21] Many seem to assume that without an explicit moral or ideological angle, an artistic depiction of something is almost always tantamount to an artist's endorsement of the same thing. A scene in a movie that depicts adultery without explicitly condemning it is a celebration of infidelity. A novel with scenes of horrific violence betrays the author's approval of horrific violence. But context is usually more telling than content.

Comedy is one artistic discipline that, when done well, makes masterful use of the complexities of context. In his *Humanity* standup special, comedian Ricky Gervais wrestled with the way that the modern fondness for offense and outrage inevitably neuters comedy. "A joke about a bad thing isn't as bad as the bad thing," he said. "It's not even necessarily condoning the bad thing. It could be *anti* the bad thing. It depends on the actual joke."[22]

If a parent warns a child against using a profane word, how else will the child understand the prohibition without knowing what the word is? Suppose, then, a parent was to say, "I do not want you to use the word *fuck*. It is an offensive word." In context, of course, it is perfectly sensible, even necessary, that this parent might use the offending word this way. The parent is effectively using it to denounce it. And yet, in art, many Christians seem to prefer a decidedly narrow moral toolbox. Denounce evil, but do not depict it. Or depict it but do so according to my subjective sensibilities of how such a thing can be appropriately depicted. Such a person, whether they realize it or not, makes a bold assumption of spiritual superiority. If I have declared something to be of corrupting potential, they assume it must be so for all people at all times.

LUST: A COMPLICATED SPECTRUM

I once entertained a friendly argument with a dear friend who scoffed at my mentioning the explicit sexuality in Song of Songs. I argued then (as I have in this book) that the presence of explicit sex poetry in the Bible must indicate that not all depictions of sexuality in art should be uniformly dismissed by disciples of Jesus. He laughed, fundamentally disagreeing that words were in any way comparable to images. To him, the idea that the inherent sinful bent of one individual might prefer the written word to the imagery of film and photography was absurd. After all, his own experience suggested otherwise. Later, I spoke with a mutual friend of ours. This other friend is a pastor, and she was counseling a woman who was struggling against a crippling addiction to pornography. What kind? Erotic fiction. Stories. With a whole Internet of depraved images at her fingertips, she preferred words.

In high school, I stumbled upon a collection of magazine clippings in a friend's desk drawer. The clippings were photos of women that this friend found titillating. None of the pictures he'd saved were of nude women. In fact, many of them were ordinarily dressed. I asked the guy why he had hoarded photos of clothed women in a drawer beneath his computer—a computer that could, after all, access an unfathomable selection of women without any clothes at all. This friend explained that, for him, the photos provided a guide for his imagination, which he preferred to photos that left nothing to the imagination at all. Of course, I would never suggest that his unconventional taste affords him the license to objectify the women in the photos just because the photos weren't pornographic, but I mention this icky exchange to make a point. It seemed that, for this guy, photographs of women with their clothes on were more titillating than everyday erotic fare he could've conjured from the Internet. These clothed photos became, for him, a kind of porn.

There is something of a joke in pop culture that the best-selling novel *Fifty Shades of Grey* belongs to a genre of its own making: "Mommy Porn." Gross. Sales figures suggest that many female readers unlikely to plumb the infinite cesspool of Internet pornography, *would* happily indulge in an explicitly pornographic novel they could purchase at their local grocery store checkout. On the other hand, statistics seem to suggest that many a squeaky-voiced hormonal male teenager, if asked, would prefer Internet porn over *Fifty Shades of Grey*. All this reminds us that what is overtly corrupting to some may not stir another person's brokenness in the same way.

Pornography is a sinister, destructive evil. Always and inherently vile and irredeemable to its filthy core, not only in its capacity to corrupt the mind and the soul, but as a global super-powered industry of injustice—human trafficking, rape, and violence against women are all routine fixtures of its satanic machinery. Of course, I denounce pornography with uniform contempt. But I mention the uniqueness of any given person's "limp" to highlight *nuance*. While watching James Cameron's Oscar-winning film *Titanic*, there will inevitably be viewers who objectify Kate Winslet's character, Rose, lingering and lusting over her nude image as Jack draws her "like one of his French girls." Other viewers will find the scene no more erotically titillating than Sandro Botticelli's famous painting *The Birth of Venus*, in which the nude Venus arrives on the seashore surfing an enormous clamshell. The troubled

moviegoer who condemns the untroubled moviegoer often high-
lights their own weakness with no real way of knowing the other's.
"I am troubled by this. How can *you* be untroubled? It must be
sin!" I honestly can't count the concerned Christians who have
declared, "I just don't see how any Christian could [enjoy a given
work of art] without sinning." The inference being, if they can't
see a way, a way must not exist.

Many others, however, have become so unconcerned with censorship that they have lapsed into a complete lack of discernment altogether. Faced with what appears to be the irresolvable ambiguity
of art's inherent evil or lack thereof, many simply adopt the
thoughtless methodology of "whatever." Anything goes. But this
too is a kind of all-or-nothing approach that denies nuance, refus-
ing to do the hard work of mature discernment. I get it. Blanket
statements are easy. Nuance is not. As a pastor, it is a far simpler
feat to instruct a congregation to avoid any and every film that
contains sexuality or nudity than it is to foster in them the kind of
mature discernment that accounts for context, content, and personal brokenness.

WHEN JESUS MET THE MPA

Consider the level of authority many Christians ascribe to The
Motion Picture Association. The MPA is a small, controversial[23]
board of viewers who assign films a rating of G, PG, PG-13, R, or
in rare cases, NC-17. Of course, the MPA can systematize its

approach to some extent (a PG-13 may, in some cases, contain a single non-sexual use of the F-word, but use the word twice, and you'll be saddled with an R). But, the MPA does not account for *context*. Meaning a scene of graphic violence intensifies the severity of a rating, regardless of the filmmaker's intent in depicting that violence. So, *Friday the 13th* is rated R, and so is *Saving Private Ryan*, and so is the "Christian movie" *Unplanned*, and so is Mel Gibson's movie about Jesus, *The Passion of the Christ*. Though most Christians likely know little about the history, makeup, or even process of the MPA, they, like most moviegoers, trust it as an institution to decide what we and our children will or will not see. For a certain viewer's sensibility, an R-rated movie is imbued with a kind of immorality. I know a young woman who winces every time she hears a string of swear words and will leave the room before the cuss count even reaches Tarantino levels. Sensitive as her ears may be, her eyes are even more delicate. Relatively bloodless PG-13 action flicks wrought with gunfire and explosions are too violent for her particular movie-going palate. But she did see *The Passion of the Christ*.

Though now controversial for a myriad of reasons that range from accusations of anti-Semitism to the director's behavior and personal character, the film's content alone was enough to warrant an R-rating "for sequences of graphic violence" when it was released in theaters back in 2004. As the title suggests, the film depicts—with creative license—the final twelve hours of Jesus' life and his execution. The film's most notorious scene graphically depicts Jesus being scourged to the brink of death. The sequence goes on for twelve painful minutes, though, in the three Gospel accounts that mention it, the scene is relegated to a single, non-descriptive verse. In John, "Then Pilate took Jesus and had him flogged."[24] Mark has a bit more: "Then some began to spit at him; they blindfolded him, struck him with their fists, and said, "Prophesy!" And the guards took him and beat him."[25] And Matthew tells us, "Then he released Barabbas to them. But he had Jesus flogged, and handed him over to be crucified."[26] The source material didn't afford Gibson a lot of detail with which to populate the scene, but what does appear in the text certainly unfolds on the screen. If one were to adapt other unsavory passages from the Bible for film, the subsequent visual horrors could likely rival the world's most notoriously reviled films.

Roger Ebert, perhaps the most well-known person to watch movies for a living, said of *The Passion of the Christ*, "The movie is 126 minutes long, and I would guess that at least 100 of those minutes, maybe more, are concerned specifically and graphically with the details of the torture and death of Jesus. This is the most violent film I have ever seen."[27] He went on to insist the movie deserved an NC-17 rating, claiming no child should be allowed to see it. Critic David Edelstein called the film "a two-hour-and-six-minute snuff movie—The Jesus Chainsaw Massacre—that thinks it's an act of faith."[28]

But in 2004, the amount of Christian support and celebration of this film can hardly be overstated. Many notable faith leaders who famously derided and condemned violent media suddenly encouraged parents to bring their children to their local theater to watch Jesus tortured on the big screen. The evangelical organization *Focus on the Family* called *The Passion of the Christ* "a stirring, reverent and significant motion picture for believers and nonbelievers alike."[29] Later that same year, they would say of *Exorcist: The Beginning*—another blood-soaked religious drama co-starring the devil—"its satanic imagery and special effects give it an oppressive feel. The constant onslaught of gore and gross-out images makes it almost too much to sit through."[30] One conservative pastor I knew described his own stringent discretion by bragging, I don't see R-rated movies unless they are about Jesus! But really, what movies are *not* about Jesus? Who decides? Or ask a few different people what kind of art they think Jesus appreciates. Does Jesus blanch at swear words? Did he enjoy Mel Gibson's adaptation of his final hours? Did Jesus find the violence of a prequel to *The Exorcist* "too much to sit through"? Maybe some people may even find it difficult to imagine Jesus enjoying movies at all—betraying a deficient view of art as purely expendable entertainment.

THE HERESY OF ART AS MERE ENTERTAINMENT

In Brad Bird's excellent film *Ratatouille*, a rat named Remy struggles to be recognized and accepted as an artist among a family of non-artists. To Remy, an aspiring chef, food is more than utilitarian. But Remy's dad disagrees: "Food is fuel. You get picky about what you put in the tank, you starve."[31] Sure, food *is* fuel, but to Remy, it's something *more*.

Not all art is meant to merely entertain in the generic sense. Some very good art is meant to upset, provoke, challenge, disrupt, and disturb. I doubt anyone would choose "entertaining" as the first adjective to describe *Schindler's List*. To treat all art as little more than popcorn entertainment makes it an easy thing to dismiss, but art is more important than a way to kill time or a product to be consumed. I don't believe that Jesus would ever willingly watch, read, or behold depictions of, say, sexual immorality for the purpose of mere entertainment. Art can entertain, but it doesn't have to. No single person should decide for everyone what qualifies as "art" and what is dismissed as "entertainment." British philosopher R. G. Collingwood would agree that some art is little more than escapism, but he allowed that other works of art stand to teach us worthwhile things about reality. He called the latter category "magic art," while the former he labeled "amusement art." Both he called art, but one seems, at least implicitly, more valuable than the other.

I have adult friends who balk at my insistence that they should put down their young adult bestsellers and read literary fiction instead.

One of them told me that he reads YA for "dumb, mindless entertainment" when he doesn't feel like "going deep or learning anything." But you can see a problem here. I'm going to go out on a limb and guess that most YA authors did not intend their work as "dumb mindless entertainment," and I'd also wager that many readers don't receive it as such. So, who says what art is magical and what art is merely amusing?

Art can serve a recreational purpose, but the total conflation of art and entertainment is devaluing and dismissive. Fireworks are entertainment. Reality TV is entertainment. Would Jesus willingly watch, read, or behold depictions of sexual immorality just to be entertained by them? No, I don't think he would. Would Jesus behold (and even appreciate) some works of art that depict or deal with sexuality in some sense? I honestly believe he would, and he does. Jesus had the highest view of the Bible of anyone I know, and the Bible contains explicit artistic sexuality. In the endless debates around a Christian approach to art and entertainment, few Bible passages are cited more often than Philippians 4v8: "Finally, brothers and sisters, whatever is true, whatever is noble, whatever is right, whatever is pure, whatever is lovely, whatever is admirable—if anything is excellent or praiseworthy—think about such things." In my conversations and debates about art, I can't count the number of times I've been clobbered with this verse, as if it was the silver bullet to eradicate all arguments in favor of art one might find offensive. So, songs with uplifting messages are "pure," but *Night of the Living Dead* is most assuredly *not pure*. But the one who wields this verse against art makes the same old presupposition: only what they deem morally appropriate in art is noble, right, pure, lovely, and admirable.

Employ this logic, and you eliminate entire passages of the Bible and many of the core teachings of Jesus. After all, if an artful approach to violence, shock, sexuality, and obscenity can under no circumstances be "pure and lovely," then we've got serious trouble. According to the delicate and easily offended, is it "pure and lovely" for Jesus to encourage men who objectify women to gouge their eyes out and amputate their own limbs? Is it "pure and lovely" for Jesus to include torture and dismemberment in his parables? Is tying yourself up and stoking a fire with feces "pure and lovely?" Are historical scenes featuring gang rape and dismemberment noble, right, and admirable? Are erotic poems about groping a lover's breasts, or about oral sex excellent and praiseworthy?

Most humans are biologically wired to understand some things as objectively lovely or admirable, and some things as not. To raise a child with self-sacrificial love is admirable; to abuse a child is not. But when it comes to art, what is lovely and admirable for one person may not be equally so for another. Art is complicated in that it can depict something that is *not* lovely or admirable to communicate something that *is*. Art can represent something that is *not* lovely nor admirable with *intentions* that are not lovely nor admirable and yet evoke in its audience a reaction that *is*.

One of the more famous prophecies in the Hebrew Scriptures is in Ezekiel 37. Ezekiel documents a dark time in Israel's history. Five years after the first Babylonian attack on Jerusalem, Ezekiel sits despairing in an Israelite refugee camp. It's his birthday and the year he would have been installed as a priest were it not for Israel's sin and punishment. Even after Ezekiel's visions and his bizarre performance art sign acts, he knows that it isn't going to work. Babylon invades Jerusalem, and the city falls. But the story doesn't end there. God promises a coming king—the king Israel has always needed—who will rule over a transformed people because God will replace their old, calloused hearts with new, soft and supple hearts that are finally capable of yielding to the loving goodness of God. All of this comes to Ezekiel as compelling and artistic visual symbols. And then things get weird.

Ezekiel finds himself in a valley littered with the decomposed remains of countless humans. These heaps of old skeletons begin to rattle and vibrate, then fasten themselves together, staggering to their bony feet. Then, as Ezekiel watches, glistening muscles and sinew snake down the bleached bones, wet eyes form in the once barren sockets.[32] What had, moments prior, been hopeless corpses, God tells Ezekiel, represent seemingly hopeless Israel. And this shocking miracle of restoration represents God's promise to restore his people. God uses morbid, grisly images to communicate the seriousness of Israel's condition and promise them hope.

FLEEING THE THEATER

In 2018, a friend of mine fled the theater during the first act of an indie arthouse flick called *Hereditary*. I found the same movie profoundly affecting, theologically astute, and emotionally devastating. Of the dozens of new movies I saw that year, it was my favorite. This friend of mine, who is not easily offended, stood up and left the theater about a half hour into the film's runtime. "I couldn't do it," he told me afterward. I think it was okay for him to leave, and I think it was okay for me to stay. We both, I think, exercised discernment.

For me, *Hereditary* was most assuredly lovely, admirable, excellent, and praiseworthy. I have often turned it over in my mind since. I have considered its horrifying images in prayer and while meditating before God. I believe that filling my mind with praiseworthy artistry shapes the person I am becoming for the better. John Calvin (of all people!)[33] argued for a Christian appreciation of "profane" art. "In reading profane authors," he said, "the admirable light of truth displayed in them should remind us, that the human mind, however much fallen and perverted from its original integrity, is still adorned and invested with admirable gifts from its Creator. If we reflect that the Spirit of God is the only fountain of truth, we will be careful, as we should avoid offering insult to him, not to reject or condemn truth wherever it appears. In despising the gifts, we insult the Giver."[34]

Once, I mentioned through an online outlet that my favorite album is *The Fragile* by Nine Inch Nails. Someone responding by asking, "How can you glorify God while listening to this?" I answered with a question. How can I *not* glorify God while listening to it? I am in awe of the God-imbued musicianship and vivid, evocative imagery. My attention is consistently drawn to the God of creativity—the original artist. I'm reminded of my own story: Sin, shame, self-loathing, despair, lament. I am drawn to worship Jesus, who saved me. I've used portions of the album for spiritual disciplines (contemplation, imaginative prayer, even worship (See "Underneath It All").

In my life, art has been one of the primary means by which God has shaped my heart to grow into the love, joy, and peace that make up the inner condition of Jesus. Some of the art that I have found to be profoundly "Christian" in this way, someone else might find offensive. If I had heeded the black-and-white advice of some who were concerned for my purity, I believe I could have severely impeded God's call over my life. Had I not read Kafka, listened to Queen, watched *The Fly*, I would not have connected with God profoundly, and understood the person he has wired me to be. Of course, there have been other occasions when I was sorely mistaken to shirk the wisdom of those close to me when they showed appropriate concern for the art I enjoy. Not every suspicion of sin is misplaced, and I have absolutely enjoyed art irresponsibly, closed off to conviction by a wall of pride and self-righteous indignation. But when I operate with thoughtful nuance, led by the Spirit of God, in submission to the Scriptures, and in cooperation with the community of God's people, I make better decisions about what I listen to and watch and read and behold, even if those decisions look a little different than some else's. I would never assume that *The Fragile* is something for all Christians to enjoy and to celebrate. To someone else, the obscenity might prove toxic, the nihilism corrupting, the abstract nature of it all confusing, even misleading.

Some Christians need to flee the theater. Others need to stay.

CHAPTER 3:3

BURN *THESE* BOOKS, NOT *THOSE* BOOKS

IN 1995, THE US Secretary of Education joined forces with the head of the National Political Congress of Black Women to take down offensive music. The pair crashed a Time Warner shareholder's meeting in New York, where they challenged company officials to read aloud the lyrics to the Nine Inch Nails song "Big Man With A Gun." The company officials declined. Later, Trent Reznor—the man responsible for "Big Man With A Gun"—told *Spin* he could sympathize with the outrage, explaining how the song had been designed to fit into the album's narrative. "To me, (the album) builds to a certain degree of madness, then it changes. That would be the last stage of delirium. So the original point of 'Big Man With A Gun' was madness. But it was also making fun of… misogynistic gangsta-rap… I could do without the degree of misogyny and hatred of women... Then, my song got misinterpreted as exactly that… I've been taken out of context, and it's ridiculous."[1]

The first time I heard "Big Man With a Gun," I was shocked. Even amidst an album overflowing with lyrical content many would find particularly transgressive, the song is jarring in its satire of hyperbolic sexualized violence. Even then, the idea that this ridiculous song was meant to be understood as the voice of the actual songwriter seemed absurd. It was a fictional narrator—an unreliable one. A cartoon. This doesn't mean that the album *The Downward Spiral* is insincere, but it does suggest that the album's narrator is not necessarily communicating the lucid and literal ideas of the songwriter who created him. The album's narrator, for example, sings, "God is dead, and no one cares" in the song "Heresy," but Trent Reznor, when asked if he believes in God, admits, "I do… I've had some dark days through the years and… that makes me think there is some reason here and it's beyond just physics and biology."[2]

Of course, that doesn't make these lyrics any less offensive. In the same interview, Reznor admitted, "I think *The Downward Spiral* actually could be harmful." *Could be* are the operative words. He didn't say so directly, but I assume Reznor intended to say that in the wrong hands—misinterpreting hands—the very words meant to condemn misogyny can be misconstrued to support it. The same songs designed to explore and confront depression and suicide can be misconstrued to celebrate and endorse them. In 1995, "Big Man With a Gun" represented the depths of depravity to which mainstream music could sink for profanity-averse conservatives, but more than two decades later, it became a sore spot for progressive

Nine Inch Nails fans. "Regardless of how he's explained its original intent," one Reddit user argued in 2022, "The track isn't just misogynistic, it's downright rapey… It's gross. No one likes it in 2022."[3] 27 years later, listeners across a broad spectrum of sensibilities still can't (or won't) conceive of song lyrics that somehow *depict* sexual violence without *endorsing* it.

Writer Ottessa Moshfegh, in her essay on the novel *Less Than Zero*, describes the complicated and vital nature of this kind of satire. "The difference between sincerity and satire is in the eye of the beholder. Someone with critical thinking can detect satire. Someone who is used to swallowing blindly whatever is served will never understand subtlety... We favour straight arrows over innuendo. This is a weakness. Satire is the most difficult mode in literature because it functions with a delicate, invisible layer of self-awareness —which readers often lack."[4]

THE FRUSTRATING SUBJECTIVITY
OF INTERPRETATION

Like art theory itself, *interpretation* is a hotly debated concept. For hundreds of years, there was some agreement in literary studies that the meaning of a written work was found exclusively in whatever the author intended to communicate. Thus, the meaning of "Big Man With A Gun" is a satire of madness and misogyny. But in the last hundred years or so, the consensus shifted. Now, literary academics and enthusiasts often argue that, once written, literature takes on a life of its own. The meaning is imbued in the work, independent of the author's intent, and the meaning shifts and changes depending on the reader, the reader's context, and the world around them.[5] This evolving understanding of art is easy to mock. Cold and narcissistic, it seems to snatch authorial intent from the equation entirely, making art a product that must yield to the consumer. The customer is always right. We get to decide! But though authorial intent has always mattered in art, but it has never been the bottom line or the final word.

The cult classic trashterpiece *Troll 2* has long been an icon of midnight movie screenings and the subject of a documentary called *Best Worst Movie*. Audiences find the writing hysterical, the effects laughable, the logic baffling. But Claudio Fragasso—the director of *Troll 2*—disagrees with the audience. When asked how it feels to have directed the worst movie ever made, Fragasso rebutted, "I did a very good movie."[6] Fragasso's intent certainly factors in how *Troll 2* is understood. The fact that the filmmaker did not intend to make a ridiculous movie is the reason audiences love it. But, the artist's creative intention cannot coerce the audience's response. He thinks it's serious; they think it's ridiculous. People experience art in wildly different ways. What inspires and edifies one person may have no effect on another. What offends and scandalizes one person may seem innocuous or irrelevant to another.

Before Todd Philipps' film *Joker* was released in 2019, people were already going bananas arguing about it. *Tell us*, they demanded, *exactly what this film means to say*! At the film's center is the unwell Arthur Fleck, played by Joaquin Phoenix, who won an Oscar and a slew of other awards for the performance. *Joker* borrows from films like *Taxi Driver* and *Raging Bull* in its character study of one lonely, unwell man's descent into violent madness. Unleashed during a season of acute political tension, the public perception of *Joker* became volatile, with many mainstream journalists suggesting boycotts.[7] Is *Joker* meant to make light of mental illness and social injustice? Does the movie condone or encourage violence? Is it a satire or a vindication of what some call "white male rage"? Is Arthur Fleck a villain or a hero? Does *Joker* condone or condemn the things it portrays? Would either thing render the film immoral? Film critic Peter Travers asked Joaquin Phoenix, "Are we meant to sympathize with [Arthur Fleck]?" Phoenix answered, "No, you're meant to feel whatever you feel."[8]

Audiences often spin their wheels in the quicksand of interpretation, but art doesn't always intend to prepackage a single objective moral position. Art can kind of just depict and comment on things in the world and leave the audience to react. This doesn't mean that art can never communicate a clear or moral message, but it does make quantifying what a given work of art will say or do to an entire audience an impossibility. It all depends on the person. Most viewers find depictions of sexual abuse disturbing, but someone who has experienced sexual abuse may find the same depictions uniquely overwhelming. Jordan Belfort's memoir (and its film adaptation) *The Wolf of Wall Street* seems ridiculous and loathsome to many, yet it incites desire, lust, and greed in others. An American audience will experience a World War II drama differently than an audience in Germany, Japan, or France. Most Western moviegoers have no idea that Godzilla was a metaphor for Hiroshima.

In an episode of the sitcom *Wings*, Brian and Helen search a video rental store, arguing about which movie is best for the evening. Helen suggests *Trading Places*, and Brian approves, saying, "Perfect! Comedy, Christmas theme, just the right amount of nudity."

"Brian," Helen objects. "There's no nudity in this film."

Brian rebuts. "Excuse me. Approximately 45 minutes in, Jamie Lee Curtis takes her top off."[9]

This exchange, played for '90s sitcom laughs, illustrates the differences in how people experience a given work of art. For Helen, the nudity in *Trading Places* was a non-event. She didn't even remember it. For Brian, it was *the* event. What one finds titillating in art will depend on a myriad of complicated factors ranging from sexual orientation, preference, wiring, and something the New Testament authors call *the flesh*. The apostle Paul calls the flesh our "cravings"[10] and "sinful passions."[11] Peter describes the flesh as "corrupt desire."[12] The flesh is a complicated tangle of every person's unique personality and innate brokenness, a propensity toward selfishness leeching off preference. So, some people are more carnal, others more materialistic. Some people struggle with melancholy, others with anger. Many battle against all of these things in varying degrees, depending on the situation and season of life. And art can *confront* the flesh, but it can also *feed* it. This is a conundrum. Art is like sex: Inherently good, created by God *for* good, but complicated, dynamic, and abused by people. Because people are capable of evil and because people make art, art can be powerfully destructive. Like sex, art is uniquely uplifting and/or devastating from one person to another, contingent on the context of a person and what's going on in their life. This renders blanket statements obsolete. In art, what feeds the flesh of one confronts the flesh of another. What challenges the flesh of one energizes the flesh of another. We know this from science, statistics, experience, and the Bible.

You can, if you want, encourage all Christians to be celibate. Celibacy, after all, is a blessed and viable option for disciples of Jesus. Paul even mentions celibacy is, in some ways, preferable to marriage.[13] While we're at it, maybe we should encourage all Christians to abstain from alcohol. That would eliminate the risk of drunkenness, which the Bible uniformly condemns as a disastrous evil. But while celibacy and teetotalism are both good—even important—decisions for some disciples of Jesus, neither are required of everyone.

I have a friend with a history of alcoholism in his family. He has an addictive personality. His dad was an abusive drunk. He has decided to abstain from alcohol altogether. He knows he doesn't have to, but that was his call. I have another friend who didn't drink at all until after his thirtieth birthday. He's never been drunk, not even close. I think it's suitable for the first friend to abstain, and I think it's suitable for the second friend to enjoy. I have a friend who paints. She's taken classes where nude models have stood for still-life paintings. I have another friend who feels so drawn to lust that he finds it challenging to sit through an episode of *Friends* without objectifying the actresses. I think it's appropriate for the first friend to paint, and I think it's appropriate for the second friend to refrain from *Friends* if he lacks the spiritual maturity to watch it without thinking of Jennifer Anniston as an object.

According to Jesus and the authors of the New Testament, many of us wholly misunderstand the true nature of freedom and slavery. In pop culture philosophy, freedom is an allowance. Meaning you are free *to do* something—drink Diet Coke, buy things, have sex, say what you want, believe whatever, do whatever. "You do you." But in the New Testament, freedom is about being released *from internal oppression*. You have been set free *from* the power of the devil, set free from *your own desire*. An idea like this is dangerously archaic in today's vernacular. If the You Do You creed is freedom, the opposite of freedom is disciplined self-denial. And that, we are told, is very bad. But anyone remotely honest about themselves and the human experience must confess that doing what you want to do isn't always great advice. As people, we often want things—*really* want things—that aren't so great. From fast food to mass murder.

Because human-made art is complicated, multifaceted, and subjective, it can be dangerous and destructive. It can fan the flames of selfish desire, incite the objectification of people made in God's image, inspire greed and idolatry, and nurture despair. The problem is that the same work that does all that for one person could do the opposite for another. The solution to modern protestant Christianity's art phobia is not *anything goes* nor *censorship*. The solution is thoughtful, nuanced discernment, submitted to the teachings of Jesus and the Scriptures, fueled by maturity in the Holy Spirit, worked out in the accountability of community with other disciples of Jesus.

THE DARK HALLWAY

Discernment is when a disciple of Jesus brings the Scriptures, wisdom, the Holy Spirit, and the community of God's people to bear on selective decisions about how to best understand and enjoy art and what to avoid for the sake of spiritual formation and faithful discipleship. *Censorship* is when a person or a group of people pass judgment on a given work of art and set out to suppress that which they find unacceptable. Thinking of this kind requires brazen arrogance. It requires the censor to presuppose their own conviction applies to all people at all times, without nuance or conversation. They become the self-appointed arbiter of art moralism. Burn *these* books, not *those* books.

Censorship has become increasingly prevalent in the ongoing debate over free speech and "safe spaces." Should we expunge Mark Twain's *The Adventures of Huckleberry Finn* or Harper Lee's *To Kill a Mockingbird* from the public record because they include racial slurs? Should we fret and protest on university campuses when they host guest speakers espousing ideologies with which we disagree? Censorship mentality is a dark hallway from which one rarely resurfaces because it invariably raises the haunting question: who gets to decide? When we agree that some art can be dangerous in specific contexts, the idea of somehow mitigating the consequences can seem appealing, but at what cost?

God, as an artist, designed his work with deadly potential. God made beings that are free, and things have obviously gone awry. For hundreds of years, all the earliest theologians and thinkers attributed the reality of evil and suffering to the autonomy of humans and spiritual beings. Meaning God was after actual relationships, actual collaboration, actual *love*—so he created human beings and spiritual beings with genuine freedom. Historically, many (if not most) disciples of Jesus have acknowledged the libertarian freedom of human beings and spiritual beings as the explanation for evil. You can argue with God about it (and people do), but God seemed to believe that the potential for real love was worth the risk.

God didn't and doesn't censor his work. Censorship imposes unambiguous moral standards on something inherently morally ambiguous: Art. If you are a disciple of Jesus, there will be some art you should likely refrain from looking at, watching, listening to, etc. But that doesn't make it wrong for everyone. It may be wrong for one person to drink because they struggle with doing so responsibly. To another, the occasional glass of wine is no big deal. For one person, dieting and fitness are healthy and responsible, but for another, both are bogged in obsessive vanity and narcissism. Even something that's usually admirable—like traveling to distant countries to do social justice— can be abused, repurposed for digital virtue signaling and image curation. Most of us understand this logic well enough but fail to apply it to the arts.

Should we ban alcohol? Discourage all dieting and exercise? Cut off missions to the majority world? Of course not. But why? All of these things, in the wrong hands, do undeniable damage to innumerable people, but the way of black-and-white moralism doesn't account for the unique conviction and constitution of the individual, and it objectifies and condemns things God designed for good. As the adage goes, the possibility of abuse does not remove the legitimacy of proper use.

REN & STIMPY, TWICE CANCELED

At the time of writing this book, there is an overwhelming surge in the American sensibility to censor anything and everything that deviates from accepted progressive groupthink. Even past works—products of their times and places—are being reevaluated and scrutinized according to ever-evolving ideological sensibilities. Songwriter Nick Cave was asked if he felt mounting pressure to alter lyrics he'd written in 1992 that undoubtedly incense fragile modern ears. He answered, "What songwriter could have predicted thirty years ago that the future would lose its sense of humour, its sense of playfulness, its sense of context, nuance and irony, and fall into the hands of a perpetually pissed off coterie of pearl-clutchers?... I would rather be remembered for writing something that was discomforting or offensive, than to be forgotten for writing something bloodless and bland."[14]

At one time, it was ordinary for thinking people to behold art and entertain ideas with which they might disagree, concluding peaceably, "I hear you, but I disagree with you." As perspectives hardened and ideologies became increasingly weaponized, their adherents increasingly militant, the creed became, "I disagree with you, so I will not hear you." Then, "I disagree with you therefore you must be silenced altogether." And finally, "I disagree with you therefore you and everything you've created must be destroyed."

"Cancel Culture" became a household term around 2017, but the whole thing was old and familiar. A couple of decades prior, the moral absolutism of the political right was outspoken and mobilized in their efforts to put an end to all art and entertainment (as well as all artists and entertainers) that did not abide by their conservative moral rulebook. This discriminating air of censorship swells beyond the art itself and engulfs the artist as well. Years later, the moral absolutism of the political left picked up where the right left off—just as outspoken, and maybe even more mobilized and ruthless in their quest to vanquish their enemies. Ren and Stimpy were on the chopping block both times.

The Ren & Stimpy show premiered in 1991 to massive fanfare and critical acclaim, quickly becoming one of the most influential animated series of all time. But when what was ostensibly a children's program dabbled openly in fart jokes, gross-out gags, violent surrealism, and gallows humor, Parents and politicians called for the show to be banned. 27 years later, Ren & Stimpy were tainted for many former fans after an article published in BuzzFeed accused the show's creator, John Kriscfalusi, of sexually grooming and abusing two underage girls.[15] A 2020 effort to reboot the characters (without Kricfalusi's involvement) was met with vocal online backlash, and a widely circulated petition calling for the reboot's cancellation before production had begun. It wasn't just John Kriscfalusi being indicted and punished for his actions; a cartoon that he made in collaboration with dozens of other artists was being held equally responsible, even if Kriscfalusi himself was no longer involved in making it.

Comedian Rowan Atkinson (who is famous for his bumbling Mr. Bean character) argued for free speech before parliament in 2012, saying, "'I am not intolerant', say many people; say many softly spoken, highly-educated, liberal-minded people: 'I am only intolerant of intolerance.' And people tend to nod sagely and say 'Oh, wise words, wise words' and yet if you think about this supposedly inarguable statement for longer than five seconds, you realize that all it is advocating is the replacement of one kind of intolerance with another. Which to me doesn't represent any kind of progress at all... For me, the best way to increase society's resistance to insulting or offensive speech is to allow a lot more of it."[16]

In 2017, the Whitney Museum of American Art in New York City displayed a painting by Dana Schutz called *Open Casket*. The painting depicts Emmett Till, who was brutally lynched by two white men in 1955. Emmett Till—a fourteen-year-old African American in Mississippi—was falsely accused of lecherous advances toward a white woman (the woman in question later admitted she had fabricated the exchange).[17] The young Till was beaten so savagely that his body was unrecognizable. His murderers were acquitted. At Emmett's funeral, his mother insisted the casket remain open so that the world would be exposed to the horror of her son's murder. Photos of Emmett Till's mangled corpse were circulated around the country, massively impacting the civil rights movement in America. *Open Casket* depicts Emmett Till in his coffin, his face a blur of smeared paint. The piece attracted controversy and outrage because Dana Schutz is a White woman. In an open letter to the museum, artist Hannah Black called not only for the immediate removal of *Open Casket* but that the painting should be "destroyed and not entered into any market or museum."[18] The letter argued, "The subject matter is not Schutz's; white free speech and white creative freedom have been founded on the constraint of others, and are not natural rights. The painting must go."[19]

In response to the well-publicized indignation, Dana Shutz claimed she had never intended to commandeer Black suffering with her piece but that the painting was born from the empathy of motherhood. She said, "I don't know what it is like to be black in America, but I do know what it is like to be a mother. Emmett was Mamie Till's only son. The thought of anything happening to your child is beyond comprehension… It is easy for artists to self-censor… To convince yourself to not make something before you even try. There were many reasons why I could not, should not, make this painting … (but) art can be a space for empathy, a vehicle for connection."[20]

Professor Coco Fusco, a Cuban-American artist whose work has dealt openly with issues of race, wrote candidly about what she argued were the dangerous implications of the backlash against *Open Casket*. "I find it alarming and entirely wrongheaded to call for the censorship and destruction of an artwork," she said. "No matter what its content is or who made it. As artists and as human beings, we may encounter works we do not like and find offensive. We may understand artworks to be indicators of racial, gender, and class privilege—I do, often. But presuming that calls for censorship and destruction constitute a legitimate response to perceived injustice leads us down a very dark path. [Those protesting *Open Casket*] are placing themselves on the wrong side of history, together with Phalangists who burned books, authoritarian regimes that censor culture and imprison artists, and religious fundamentalists who ban artworks in the name of their god."[21]

When you begin to censor art that offends some, or when you scrub the record of art made by "bad" people, you eventually arrive with *no art*. Ricky Gervais once said, "That's what the world is like. People see something they don't like, and they expect it to stop, as opposed to dealing with their own emotions."[22] A friend of mine once confided that in his effort to become a more racially sensitive White man, he'd become uncomfortable singing a popular worship song that employed imagery from Isaiah 1v18 with the lyric, "Though our sins are scarlet, you've made us white as snow." Well-meaning and empathetic, he wondered if the song should be retired, the lyrics adjusted. Ultimately, it was a conversation about censoring the Bible based on a very literal reading of a very figurative piece of writing. So why end there? What else should change? What other sensibilities should be taken into consideration? At what point do those sensibilities become the sole engine that drives the creative process?

When Oprah Winfrey selected the Jeanine Cummins novel *American Dirt* for her book club in 2020, the social media outrage was instantaneous. *American Dirt* tells the story of a Mexican woman fleeing cartel violence as she makes for the border with her sons. Though *American Dirt* depicts Mexico and Mexicans, the author is a White American. Cummins was accused of "brownface," and her publisher canceled a planned book tour, citing threats against the author's life. Despite overwhelming pressure to denounce the novel, Oprah followed the dangerous logic to its inevitable conclusion, arguing, "I fundamentally believe in the right of anyone to use their imagination and their skills to tell stories. If one author... one artist is silenced, we're all in danger of the same. I believe that we can do this without having to cancel, to dismiss or to silence anyone."[23] In 2017, the Swedish music streaming platform Spotify removed an array of acts from its service when they were deemed "hate bands."[24] Later, this policy was expanded to consider not just the lyrical content of artists but also the artist's real-life behavior.[25] Censorship of this kind becomes an immediate labyrinth of hypocrisy and absolutism. Who decides what makes a "hate band"? Is it the inclusion of racial slurs? Can racial slurs be used satirically? Who decides what qualifies as irony? Who decides what kind of personal behavior qualifies an artist for censorship or disqualifies them from making art? *American History X* is a film universally understood to condemn white supremacy, but it unflinchingly depicts white supremacists saying and doing extremely racist, violent things. Is the film itself hateful?

In their review of the animated film *The Secret Life of Pets 2*, *The Wrap* condemned a cartoon about talking dogs because it depicted its background human character, Katie, marrying a man and having a baby. "*The Secret Life of Pets 2*," the review argued, "effectively acts as an animated ode to heteronormativity, toxic masculinity and patriarchal worldviews, passed off as harmless plot points to entertain young audiences."[26]

Is *The Secret Life of Pets 2* a "hate movie"? Who decides?

CHAPTER 3:4

THE IMAGE OF GOD AS A VANDALIZED PAINTING

THE MORNING I SET out to write this chapter, I read a review of a neo-noir crime thriller called *Dragged Across Concrete*. The journalist described the film as "a nasty, nihilistic nightmare designed to provoke."[1] He suspected the director had made creative decisions purely to antagonize audiences. "*Dragged Across Concrete* might be one of the most unpleasant films in recent memory... And yet I cannot deny that *Dragged Across Concrete* works. In terms of content, it's a terrible film. In terms of craft, it's nothing short of remarkable... The writer-director has set out to tell a story about terrible people in a terrible world, and he's succeeded."[2] This got me thinking about Roger Ebert and the 1915 film *The Birth of a Nation*.

The Birth of a Nation is easily one of the most controversial films of all time. The silent 1915 epic is criticized for its historical inaccuracies and credited for inspiring the reformation of the Ku Klux Klan. *The Birth of a Nation* is also recognized as groundbreaking and innovative in the medium of film. In a quote that summarizes much of the spirit of this entire book, Roger Ebert said: "*The Birth of a Nation* is not a bad film because it argues for evil... it is a great film that argues for evil. To understand how it does so is to learn a great deal about film, and even something about evil."[3]

How can an artist set out to argue for evil and somehow create a great work of art in the process? How can one recognize a great work of art while also understanding its purpose is to do evil? If those responsible for *The Birth of a Nation* were clearly racist, how can we appreciate their art? This conversation took on a decidedly different tone when a new movie bearing the same name was released in 2016. The new *Birth of a Nation* tells the story of Nat Turner, an enslaved preacher who leads an uprising against white slavers in 1831 Virginia. To subvert the infamous 1915 film's racist propaganda by using its title to describe a story of slave insurrection seemed a fitting irony until a new detail pierced the narrative. In 1999, writer and director Nate Parker was accused of rape before being acquitted of all charges in 2001, though the incident would be hotly debated for years to come. Renewed interest in the incident cast a long shadow over his 2016 version of *The Birth of a Nation*. Many moviegoers and film journalists were unable or unwilling to separate the film from the scandal surrounding the filmmaker. Actress Gabrielle Union, who stars in the movie, criticized Nate Parker while arguing for the importance of the film itself.

A similar conversation surrounded Bill Cosby's work after the once-beloved comedian was exposed as a serial rapist. On *The Late Show,* Stephen Colbert asked comedian Jerry Seinfeld, who had most inspired his career. Seinfeld answered without hesitation: "*The* comedian was Bill Cosby... The greatest body of work, I think, in comedy, is his."[4] Colbert agreed. "I grew up on his stuff. I think he saved my life."[5] But then Colbert asked Seinfeld an interesting question. In light of Cosby's criminal charges, could Seinfeld still listen to his comedy? Seinfeld answered without hesitation, Yes. Colbert, on the other hand, could not. "I can't listen to it now… I can't separate it. Because there's love there."[6] I think what Colbert meant was that because he had taken Cosby's work so personally, because it was so formative, he felt a sting of betrayal in Cosby's crimes, and that sting has since reshaped his understanding of Cosby's work. Colbert's inability to listen to Cosby makes sense to me. But so does Seinfeld's willingness to go on enjoying it.

The disciple of Jesus imports their unique worldview into their understanding of art and artists. In the worldview of Jesus, human beings are broken. Bent out of shape. Flawed. Capable of good and capable of evil. For centuries, Christians have accepted this in our reading and understanding of King David. We love to point out that though David's flaws dwarf those of the average reader, he is yet described as "a man after [God's] own heart."[7] In one of

David's most infamously depraved moments, he stands on a roof-top, ogling a bathing woman called Bathsheba. Though he knows her to be married, David sends for her and has sex with her (some Bible scholars argue that David raped Bathsheba).[8] She becomes pregnant, and rather than confront the consequences of his actions, God's appointed king of Israel manipulates his subjects, using military strategy to see that Bathsheba's husband is killed. Later, the Holy Spirit inspired David to write a song that captures some of his grief over the whole thing.[9] We still use this song today to pray and to learn. We do the same with dozens of other songs written by David. We know that David abused his God-given power to satiate his lust and cover over his evil, that he objectified and abused a woman made in God's image, that he murdered her husband. Knowing all of this complicates our relationship with David's art, but it doesn't make David's art less beautiful or less meaningful. David's brokenness imbues his art with a unique dimension of meaning.

When an artist creates something, that work is paradoxically tethered to that artist while simultaneously taking on a life all its own. We know this to be true because we often (if not mostly) receive and experience art without any knowledge or detailed understanding of the artist who created it. Most of the casual movie-going public doesn't know who directed the movie they saw on Saturday night, let alone a laundry list of all the director's sin and character defects. Everyone knows the chorus of "We Are the Champions," but few people can name all the members of Queen. The average museum guest strolls past painting after painting without researching the names mounted beside them. Art is irrevocably tethered to the artist while yet inhabiting a world in which the artist can become inconsequential to the art. Historically, artists are, more often than not, a complicated people. Artists can be neurotic, obsessive, melancholy, extreme, self-obsessed (and thus, self-loathing), and moody. An artist, by nature, must reject homogeneity. If they do not, they are likely more like craftsmen or entertainment capitalists than artists. Since an artist tends to disregard the status quo, they often find themselves at odds with it. And all artists are deeply flawed.

The creative process for which the artist was ordained by God has been disrupted by the artist's brokenness. When one creates, they always mirror the Creator, at least in the sense that they create. But unlike the Creator, we can only do it so well. And when we do it, shades of our brokenness likely permeate or even vandalize our creations. Even so, we go on creating upon the ordination of God. Artists who do not know or care for the things of Jesus *can* create beautiful and noteworthy things, and deeply devout disciples of Jesus can create toxic and destructive things. When God is the Creator, the creative work is always good. When we do it, it's a bit more complicated.

Adolph Hitler was an artist. He painted. His paintings are pretty good. Serial killer John Wayne Gacy also painted, and his paintings are pretty bad in the technical sense but interesting and noteworthy because a serial killer painted them. There has never been a single work of human art created by an artist who was not guilty of evil. Artists, as with all humans, sin. They do heinous things. Sometimes, they take responsibility, make amends, repent. Sometimes they do not. But the search for the guiltless artist and their guiltless art is a hopeless cause. If I discovered today that Franz Kafka had been a mass murderer, I can't change the fact that his book *The Metamorphosis* inspired me to write fiction when I was eleven years old. All rational humans must agree that even very evil people can be talented, intelligent, enterprising, and creative. It logically follows that artists who are "bad people" can create "good art." Both versions of *The Birth of a Nation* may be, in some sense, "good" as feats of filmmaking go. This is true even if the filmmakers are guilty of evil. That doesn't mean you have to like the movies or the behavior of the people who made them, but there you go.

When accepting the Mark Twain Prize for American Humor, Dave Chapelle celebrated the medium of comedy, understanding that comedians and their ideas can themselves be disagreeable. As a Black comic who favors sociopolitical commentary over props or observational humor, Chapelle admitted, "I know comics that are very racist... I don't get mad at them, don't hate them. We go upstairs and have a beer. And sometimes I even appreciate the artistry that they paint their racist opinions with." If an artist says something true in their art, it doesn't stop being true when we learn the artist has also done bad things. If an artist creates something praiseworthy in its craftsmanship, its craftsmanship doesn't cease to be praiseworthy when we learn the artist is imperfect or even guilty of evil.

We could spend the rest of this book citing examples. Jerry Lee Lewis, one of the more prominent figures in rock music, married his thirteen-year-old first cousin when he was 22. Dr. Seuss is perhaps the most noteworthy figure in children's literature; he also drew racist political cartoons that feature the N-word as a punch line. Roman Polanski directed classic films like *Rosemary's Baby* and *The Pianist*; he was also arrested for the sexual assault of a 13-year-old. Caravaggio was one of the most influential Italian Renaissance painters of the 17th century; he also killed a man during an attempt to castrate him. Virginia Wolf and T.S. Eliot were anti-Semites. Dickens was allegedly a lousy dad. Norman Mailer tried to kill his wife with a penknife.

Journalist Russel Smith wrote: "The great Renaissance sculptor and goldsmith Benvenuto Cellini, creator of *Perseus With the Head of Medusa,* was a murderer and a rapist. He killed at least two men and was accused by a model of sexually assaulting her. This does not stop me from looking with great amazement and curiosity at the naked and sexual Perseus With the Head of the

Medusa… I assume that all art is made by people who are pretty bad in one way or another and that I am going to see the world through the prism of their own particular badness. I assume that any good art will be in part about badness."[10] Smith's observation is a clarifying lens for those who follow Jesus: All art is created by broken people. No art remains unscathed by the brokenness of the artist. The inexorable badness of artists and the way that badness often suffuses their art does not make observing or even admiring that art a bad thing to do. Smith goes on to ask, "Even if I read a book that is explicitly about child abuse and that appears to be unjudgmental about child abuse (*Lolita*, say), am I perpetuating it or just trying to understand the deeply bad world? …Art can be propagandistic, yes, but I am an adult with a critical faculty, not just a pulsing irrational emotional sensor; I can think and analyze what I read and see… Eliminate the bad artists from the canon and you might as well eliminate art itself."[11]

If we want to understand and appreciate art, there's no way around it: all art comes from messed-up people. One journalist summarized it this way: "Accepting that doesn't mean excusing horrible private behavior. It doesn't mean giving my money to people I find reprehensible. And it doesn't mean that creative geniuses are übermenschen beyond the moral laws that govern mere mortals. It just means realizing that not every movie I love is great, and not every great movie is one I want to see. And sometimes great artists are going to be people I really don't like."[12]

I was at a party once when a song by The Smiths began playing from a stereo somewhere in the background. A young girl looked up at the man beside her and asked, "Dad, what song is this? I like it!" The Father corrected his daughter. "No, honey. That's Morrissey singing. He's a racist and a jerk. This song is not good." The girl walked away, looking confused. Could it not be true that Morrissey might be a jerk, *and* the song was also good?

AMY GRANT: REDUX

If Amy Grant's foray into mainstream pop wasn't enough to draw scorn from the Christian music machine, her divorce certainly got the job done. In 1999, Grant ended her first marriage and, one year later, began her second. I have a close friend who grew up in the Christian culture bubble. Her family was torn apart by a traumatic divorce, and the experience has had a significant impact that ripples through her story and her family to this day. For a long time, this friend of mine felt unable to enjoy or appreciate Amy Grant because of her controversial public divorce.

Upon learning this, I chastised my friend. Why hold Amy's divorce against her? Regardless of how my friend felt about Amy Grant's love life, *Heart in Motion* is an incredible album. It only occurred to me much later that my friend's aversion to Amy's music had less to do with any ideological stance and more to do with the way news of Amy's divorce arrived in the midst of my friend's own personal tragedy. And while a singer's divorce isn't an indication of their artistic capabilities, my friend was entirely free to pass on Amy Grant. I'm free to enjoy her music. Stephen Colbert is free to get rid of his old Bill Cosby records. Jerry Seinfeld is free to go on listening to them. No one is obligated to watch either version of *The Birth of a Nation* if they don't want to. They can see them both if they so choose. Doing one thing isn't necessarily more or less moral than the other.

Just as any given work of art might offend someone, so too might any given artist. That's the nature of people and art. Many people find the animated TV series *The Ren & Stimpy Show* outrageous and offensive for its black comedy and innuendo. Others, because the show's creator, John Kricfalusi, has been accused of creating a volatile and abusive work environment and sexually exploiting teenage girls. Even so, *The Ren & Stimpy Show* is widely accepted as one of the most groundbreaking and influential cartoons of all time, and many have cited John Kricfalusi as an artistic genius unparalleled in his field.[13]

Today, the backlash against the crimes of an artist often results in campaigns to scrub the world of their impact. Following the release of the *Leaving Neverland* documentary, an already divided public opinion about the late pop superstar Michael Jackson became further clouded with controversy. The documentary centers around two men who allege that, while they were children,

Jackson sexually abused them. In response, the producers of *The Simpsons* removed an episode that featured Michael Jackson's voice acting (albeit uncredited) from all TV and streaming platforms, as well as future home video releases. Radio stations around the world began to remove Jackson's music from their playlists. Michael Jackson's music hadn't changed, but the way the world experienced it at that time had. For many, to sit through hours of graphic descriptions of child molestation at the hands of Michael Jackson and then put on *Thriller* simply makes no sense. I sympathize. Simpsons producer James L. Brooks decided to "erase" the now-infamous Michael Jackson episode because he suspected Jackson may have used his Simpsons connection to groom young boys for abuse. "I'm against book burning of any kind," he said. "But this is our book, and we're allowed to take out a chapter."[14]

As with works of art, blanket statements about how all audiences should receive artists fall short. The effort to cleanse the world of art created by bad people ultimately cleanses the world of art itself. But that doesn't mean that to respect art, we must accept all of it without any consideration for the artist's life or behavior, regardless of our own experiences and sensibilities. The idea isn't to readily dismiss anything remotely offensive to the fragile and unthinking, nor is it to approach all art and all artists with an "anything goes" mentality. The idea is wise and mature discernment—informed by the Scriptures, tested by the Holy Spirit, and worked out in the accountability of God's people. We enter this process presupposing the outcome is often complicated and subjective. This work can only be accomplished within a baseline understanding of art as something always created by artists and artists as always inherently imperfect.

Even history's most notorious villains are, like all humans, a mixed bag. Even horrible people are capable of doing the occasional good thing. When a person has been exposed for some terrific misdeed, we prefer to imagine them as pure evil rather than frustratingly complicated. Early on in *Leaving Neverland*, one of Michael Jackson's accusers, Wade Robson, says of Michael: "He helped me tremendously. He helped me with my career. He helped me with my creativity, with all of these sorts of things. And he also sexually abused me. For seven years."[15]

In a *New York Times* piece, Charles McGrath notes, "In the case of the artist, badness or goodness is a moral quality or judgment; in the case of his art goodness and badness are terms of aesthetic merit, to which morality does not apply… Not only can a 'bad' person write a good novel or paint a good picture, but a good picture or a good novel can depict a very bad thing."[16]

There's no doubt that the writing of Ernest Hemingway is among the most significant contributions to all of literature, and he won the Nobel Prize in 1954. But when Hemingway's youngest son thought of his Father, he wrote, "When it's all added up, papa, it will be: he wrote a few good stories, had a novel and fresh approach to reality and he destroyed [his children and wife]. Which do you think is the most important, your self-centered shit, the stories or the people?" An even more complicated example is beloved author Charles Dickens, a man credited as a social reformer and philanthropist. A professing Christian, Dickens wrote and spoke of Jesus often. He even penned a short book about Jesus just to share his faith with his children. Two monumental figures in literature—Leo Tolstoy and Fyodor Dostoyevsky—called Dickens "that great Christian writer." Remembered as a champion of the poor, Dickens even used his money to found and manage a school and shelter for prostitutes. And yet, not unlike Hemingway, this is not how his own children remember him. Dickens's daughter Katie wrote, "He did not care a damn what happened to any of us. Nothing could surpass the misery and unhappiness of our home."[17]

Was Dickens a good artist or a bad man? It seems like he was both in varying degrees across the complicated span of his imperfect life. When you read *A Christmas Carol* or *Great Expectations*, are you reading the work of a master or a monster? Sort of both. People make art and people are broken, imperfect, capable of evil. Even so, evil people can be talented and capable of complicated thought and emotion, so they sometimes create effective and impacting works of art. The life and actions of an artist impact those who receive their art in different ways. For various and valid reasons, some may find something of personal value in art created by a "bad" person. Still, others may find their knowledge of the artist's evil taints their ability to receive what their art offers. Both reactions are inevitable and both can be sensible when reached thoughtfully and without absolutism. Those who find something valuable in the art of a bad person should not be condemned or dismissed by those who do not, nor vice versa.

Because all art is created by imperfect people, any art enjoyed or admired, or valued by anyone is always over and against any bad thing the artist has ever done. That's all we've got.

CHAPTER 3:5

THE COST OF CREATION

IN MY OFFICE HANGS a framed print by illustrator Daniel Danger. It's called "Where Do You Go When You Go?" The wide, rectangular piece depicts an old wooden house set on a snowy horizon. Two upstairs windows are lit, but the rest of the house is dark. Stretching out before the house is a trail of footprints in the snow, and in the distance, the shape of a person hovers in the air above them. Before I hung this piece in my office, I was sitting with a friend. I was telling her about the ways my therapist had been helping me understand my wiring and disposition. Through those conversations, I had grown to accept that I will always be a person who feels things very deeply but that I don't have to let those deeply felt things destroy me. My friend told me that she admired this about me. "For you, there's no integrity in something unless you feel it all the way," she said. "I think part of you needs to be able to go out into The Dark Place." (The Dark Place was my way of describing a bout of emotional turmoil.) "But my prayer," she continued, "Is that God would give you a refuge while you're in The Dark Place. So that you can roam in safety, knowing your way back home." When I saw Daniel Danger's illustration, I thought of that conversation with my friend. I decided to hang it on my wall. I know that the artist did not have my story or my inferred meaning in mind when he created it, and though I appreciate his intent, this is what his piece means to me and what I remember when I see it. Almost every creative thing I have ever done has been crafted while inhabiting The Dark Place or drawing from memories of being there. For me, The Dark Place is not good or bad in and of itself, but it is a heightened state in which one feels deeply. To draw from this place—not unlike exercise or education or spiritual formation—is costly.

In the divisive film *The House that Jack Built*, the protagonist (who is a serial killer) describes his passage from one "project" to another as a kind of dealing with pain and release. He likens the experience to walking beneath a series of lampposts. Beneath a single lamp, his shadow is most dense and most contained beneath him, and as he proceeds, his shadow lengthens before him like a visual embellishment of his satisfaction. But as he continues, the shadow *behind* him begins to appear like a phantom of pain and insatiable desire. An irresolvable empty. As the shadow of satisfaction recedes, the shadow of pain stretches out until he passes directly beneath the next post, and both are confined beneath him again. Writer/director Lars von Trier uses his film's narrator to unpack this analogy of his desire to murder, but a second character in the film rightly argues that the image has a wide host of applications—including the need to create rather than destroy. The experience of creation can be uplifting, joyous, celebratory. It can also be painful, cathartic, harrowing.

For nearly two decades, I was a professional musician. When your job is music, one of the most ordinary and expected package deals of the role is to be discredited by the people around you.

"When will you get a *real* job?"
"When will you grow up?"
"Yeah, but do you make any money?"
"This is fine for now, but what *next*?"

I had been so thoroughly indoctrinated in the devaluing of my work that, subconsciously, I'd been taught to agree with it. I used to say things like, "I know it's not a *real* job, but…" I believed then and now that God had, in a certain sense, called me to do this work as a musician, but that seemed somehow insufficient in the din of being constantly vocationally discredited. I came to believe, however subtly, that the primary reason for my vocation was because, selfishly, I liked it, and it was fun. Because I liked it and because I occupied no office nor received any consistent salary, it did not qualify as "real work" in the mind of virtually everyone I knew. But being a professional musician isn't always fun. For two decades, my band and I fulfilled the roles of managers, accountants, business owners, booking agents, designers, publicists, drivers, promoters, and administrators. All this in addition to our primary vocation as writers, musicians, and performers. We were on the phone every day with agents, licensors, screen printers, A&R directors, record labels. We planned itineraries and led caravans. We charted courses and followed atlases long before the days of readily accessible GPS. We slept on floors, in vans, at rest stations. We piled into hotel rooms, survived on a daily allotment of $5 (or less), shook hands, gave autographs, posed for photos, negotiated contracts, argued with executives and designers and caterers. And through it all, at the center of this insane job, we made art. I've had other "jobs" before and after my work in the music industry, but none have been as grueling, demanding, or complex. Few people could handle it.

Life on the road—the relentless schedule, the overwhelming amount of personal sacrifice necessary to make it work—chewed people up and spit them out. But a small few of us persevered, worked insane hours, drove insane distances, and submitted our bodies and minds to meet these extraordinary and often thankless demands. And then I'd come home and let people tell me what I was doing wasn't work. I thought these other people who inhabited offices from nine to five were doing *real* work. I let them tell me that what I was doing was a glorified hobby, a fantasy world, doomed and immature, easy street. Some of my most dismissive critics were other followers of Jesus.

I was convinced that God had guided me into my vocation as an artist (though I lacked the theological language to describe it as such then). Evidence of God's gracious use of my art was everywhere, despite my long list of screw-ups and my best efforts to make my work about me. God asked me to do it, enabled me to do it, and then did some extraordinary things with it. Even so, most of the other disciples of Jesus in my life encouraged me to do something else, something I'd not been asked by God to do, but that met a more traditional American career standard.

Many Christians do not value art, so they do not appreciate artistry as a calling over an artist's life. Many Christians have assumed an understanding of art as peripheral and ultimately unimportant— little more than expendable entertainment. How then should they understand someone who claims to be appointed by God to create art? Foolish? Misled? Unrealistic? Immature? Pursuing a career in art is rarely lucrative (especially when maintaining artistic integrity), but disciples of Jesus are not asked to value or seek financial comforts. Some artistic vocations require unconventional schedules and routines, but disciples of Jesus are not expected to weigh their callings against conventional norms. In his book *Art Needs No Justification*, Hans R. Rookmaaker writes, "The Christian artist's problems are often greater… he often lacks the support of his own community, his church and family. To them he seems to be a radical or an idle no-gooder… the Christian artist today is working under great stress."[1] In the Bible and throughout church history,

God has appointed different people with different tasks. In one of his letters to the church in Corinth, Paul talks about the way that every disciple of Jesus is uniquely enabled to act as a conduit of God's Spirit and to realize God's calling over their lives.

> The eye cannot say to the hand, "I don't need you!" And the head cannot say to the feet, "I don't need you!" On the contrary, those parts of the body that seem to be weaker are indispensable, and the parts that we think are less honorable we treat with special honor. And the parts that are unpresentable are treated with special modesty, while our presentable parts need no special treatment. But God has put the body together, giving greater honor to the parts that lacked it, so that there should be no division in the body, but that its parts should have equal concern for each other. If one part suffers, every part suffers with it; if one part is honored, every part rejoices with it. (1 Corinthians 12v21-26)

To God, each member of David's 4,000-person orchestra played an important role. Each trumpeter to soundtrack the bizarre spectacle of Temple sacrifice was crucial. Every sculptor, painter, and woodworker to furnish the Tabernacle was asked by God to do so. Though the significance of their work—its impact—may have seemed unexceptional then or now.

Not everyone who *wants* to be an artist *can* or *should* be an artist. As we've already seen in the Bible, God appoints and commissions certain people (not everyone) for a life of artistry. How one receives the communicative power of a given work of art is entirely subjective, but the technical craftsmanship of a work of art is not. This isn't to say that art must adhere to manmade guidelines of quality to achieve validity—some excellent and influential art is chaotic, unrefined, "amateurish." But that doesn't mean that anyone who wants to make art can do it. Such a mentality devalues art *and* artists, and artists need us to value the God-given call on their lives. May we equip them to go out and create—the good, the bad, and the ugly.

The cost of creating is already high enough without scorn from the body of Christ. Emotions are heightened; tapping into and exploring the highs and lows of the human experience is a costly way of life. The work of the artist is desperately necessary inside and outside the Church. As the people of the original Artist himself, it falls on the church to authorize, equip, and empower others to create, and to create well. Philip Graham Ryken observed that "It is never easy to be a painter, a poet, a musician, or any other kind of artist. While every calling has unique trials and tribulations, the life of the artist especially hard… If anything, things are even more difficult for Christian artists… Christian artists often feel like they have to justify their existence. Rather than providing a community of support, some churches surround them with a climate of suspicion."[2] When the church shackles the artists among them with the rigorous and subjective rulebook of cultural Christianity, they effectively stifle the work of God himself. To what rulebook, then, would we have the artist adhere? Well… none.

Rob Zombie is a musician and filmmaker infamous for depicting explicit violence, sexuality, and satanic imagery. When asked if he suspects the things he depicts fictitiously could inspire real-life violence or satanism, Zombie said something interesting. "I don't think the rules of real life apply to art… The rules of life are different, but for fiction there can't be rules."[3] I think Rob is on to something. Art has no rules. It is not safe. It does not accommodate preference nor bow to sensitivity. Oblivious to trigger warnings, art refuses to honor safe spaces and ever-evolving cultural sensibilities. Art can be redemptive, responsible, socially conscious, sensitive, positive, uplifting… But it doesn't have to be. Art can (and often should) be offensive, outrageous, painful, scary, and upsetting. Art encompasses the entire spectrum of human experience and invites us into the place of pain as often as the place of joy. In both places, we stand to better understand what it means to be human. God is in both places. Art records moments in time, and God is in every moment.

When my son gets upset, he draws pictures. Pictures of crying faces or angry faces or breaking hearts. According to the unspoken

Christian art rulebook, my son's emotional scrawling should include some kind of redemptive conclusion, but they're just sad, twisted faces on a sheet of paper. These works of art are snapshots of feelings and moments, not exhaustive, conclusive statements about all of my son's life. I don't scold my son and ask him to add some happy faces; I recognize these images as truthful things.

JESUS QUOTED A RAPIST

On the cross—mid execution—Jesus decided to quote a poem. It's the opening line of Psalm 22: "My God, my God, why have you forsaken me?" It's a psalm of David—a psalm written by a murderer and a rapist, and Jesus quotes this lyricist during one of the most sacred moments the world has ever known. Psalm 22 *does* have some hopeful stanzas that come a bit later, but Jesus doesn't quote those sections. His quote begins and ends on a despairing, unresolved note of agony. Because God comes to us in art that encourages and in art that despairs. To focus entirely on one is to overlook the other. "Christian" art, it seems, is often concerned with avoiding pain rather than acknowledging it. Andy Crouch wrote, "There is a kind of art that is too easy, too willing to let us off the hook, too comforting and too culpably ignorant of what exactly grace costs. At the moment, we find this most often in the bestselling art of the Christian subculture than in the secular art worlds."[4] The more I follow Jesus, the more I become convinced of just how much our spiritual formation hinges on our willingness to follow Jesus into pain. Art can help us do this. Medieval

Christian artists developed a tradition called *memento mori* (Latin for "remember that you must die")—visuals like skulls, rotting fruit, and wilting flowers were incorporated in portraits and still life paintings as subtle reminders to the beholder that death is inevitable. The idea was to instill in the onlooker a sense of humility. You may have money or possessions or status, but you will die.

So will you, dear Reader. Die, that is.

These artists found an occasion to offer an essential and sobering reminder via their paintings, and they painted a whole lot of skulls and dead flowers. The Christian tendency to impose "good vibes only" doesn't just discredit much of the human experience; it stymies a significant vehicle for spiritual formation. Thus, the strange insistence on overtly redemptive art must be stricken from the rule book—the rule book itself must be destroyed.

But just because art is without rules doesn't mean the artist should maintain unchecked creative freedom. Not if they follow Jesus, anyway. Because the disciple of Jesus is not their own. Over and against the modern religious credo of "do what makes you happy," the disciple's entire life is brought under the authority of Jesus. This means that, for the artistic disciple of Jesus, every creative whim must be carried out in submission to a master. Left to their own devices—their own flesh—an artist often becomes painfully self-obsessed. Their art becomes sensual and depraved, wallowing in all manner of self-indulgence. Examples of this are everywhere. But when a disciple of Jesus creates art, they must explore the self without bowing to it. They must dissect and depict that which is sinful without participating in it. This can only be accomplished when the artist is submitted to the teachings of Jesus, operating in Spirit-led discernment, and weighed out in the accountability of community. Accountability must act as a set of protective guard-rails but never as a unilateral artistic compass. The community of God participates in the life of the artist and in their journey of spiritual formation so that every aspect of the artist's life is consistently submitted to Jesus. But an artist's community cannot become the final arbiter of an artist's work.

Controversial novelist Bret Easton Ellis was once asked how often he considers the reader during his writing process. He answered, "I don't think about the reader. Ever. And I don't care. The reader is me."[5] Mr. Ellis is not a disciple of Jesus, and though his remarks often seem purposefully designed to provoke, there's enduring wisdom here for every artist. Worrying about the audience cripples and destroys creativity.

Thing is, when an artist is fully submitted to Jesus, empowered by God's Spirit, and carrying out their discipleship within the context of community, it is still likely that they will create art that many find shocking, offensive, or obscene. I believe it's essential that some do. When the artist is concerned for or compelled by an audience—ever fretful of the audience's reaction—they embody a kind of dishonesty in their work. They say only what they think the audience wants them to say. They censor what they think the audience isn't prepared to receive. They sanitize that which offends and simplify that which challenges. They cater to expectations and existing norms, and this, in a nutshell, is the death of Christian art. Concern for the audience also stewards the lust for profit and acclaim. There is an equation in artistic expression: You can water down the creativity of an artistic message to the degree that it becomes palatable for a wide audience. The more watered down, the more comprehensible. The more comprehensible, the wider the audience. But there's a catch. The more watered down, the weaker the message for those with "ears to hear." The more creatively uninhibited the message, the more communicative power it holds for an audience prepared to receive it. The more watered down, the less power.

And so, in art, one of the chief ends of the artist is creative freedom. One of the great struggles of art and commerce is the intervention of those who would water it down. Movie studios, censors, record labels, managers, publishers, and so on. Because when money is involved, the wider the audience, the better. But a credible artist is more often most concerned with the uncompromised realization of their vision, whether it communicates to *everyone* or not. The more divisive and alienating a work of art for the *masses*, the more potent its efficacy on a particular audience.

You can dilute a piece's alienating qualities, but not without diluting its power for the audience intended to receive it in the first place. This is why designer Tibor Kalman famously argued for making things look wrong. "We live in a society and a culture and an economic model that tries to make everything look right… Look at computers. Why are they all putty-colored…? You make something off-white or beige because you are afraid to use any other color - because you don't want to offend anybody. But by definition, when you make something no one hates, no one loves it."[6]

Pandering to the expectations and sensibilities of the widest audience might be a great way to steward brand equity and move units, but it's not the best way to challenge, provoke, or truly engage the audience. Nick Cave said it well. "Challenging music, by its very nature, alienates some fans whilst inspiring others, but without that dissonance, there is no conversation, there is no risk, there are no tears and there are no smiles, and *nobody* is moved and *nobody* is affected!… In the end, to challenge our fans is to love them, even if it means losing them."[7]

Jesus himself crafted his message with the same shrewd creative precision. He realized that his audience included the hostile, the closed-off, the hard-hearted. But it also included the eager, the perked ear, the supple hearted. The latter crowd, Jesus knew, would pour over his words, investigate them for hidden meaning, and apply them to the fertile soil of their own lives. And to that other crowd? Jesus's words only frustrated them. Theologian Stanley Hauerwas observed, "Jesus uses *some* of the parables to instruct the crowd and *all* the parables to instruct the disciples."[8]

The creative disciple of Jesus must understand that their art will resonate with some and be rejected by others. Their art might profoundly affect a few, while others react with profound indifference. What stirs the soul and invites the presence of God for one will provoke the scorn and conjure the ire of another. None of this should come as any surprise to anyone familiar with the teachings of Jesus. For the disciple, popularity is, at best, a baleful omen and, at worst, a lethal poison. I believe every artist who follows Jesus should apply his teaching on costly discipleship to their vocation as artists. If your master warns, "everyone will hate you because of me,"[9] then overwhelming acclaim—without reproval—is probably a bad sign. A.W. Tozer wrote, "Nowhere in my reading of history have I ever discovered that what was popular with the crowd was right. In most instances most great men and women of God had to lean against the wind of popularity. The cost for their advancement was their popularity."[10]

When an artist ladles on the diluting water of audience expectation, compelled by the approval of the crowd, they dishonor their craft and its creator. Art becomes, at best, a compromised shade of what it might have been and at worst, an utterly disingenuous exercise in pandering. Sure, an artist could make money doing this. And hey, it feels good to be admired more than besmirched. Monk and theologian Thomas Merton once wrote a prayer that included artists. He asked of God, "Keep me from the dead works of vanity and the thankless labor in which artists destroy themselves for pride and money and reputation."[11] Creative freedom for the disciple of Jesus is the costly willingness to create that which will not always be admired by everyone. On the other hand, creative freedom is not unchecked permission for the artist to pursue their every creative whim.

THE IDOL MEAT PROBLEM

In Paul's first letter to the church in Corinth, he addresses a unique cultural conflict involving the meat of animals that had been sacrificed to pagan gods. Corinth was a pantheistic city with many deities that required the blood of animals to be appeased. Of course, the meat from an animal sacrifice had to end up *somewhere*, and in the case of the ancient Greco-Roman world, what was left was typically sold at the local market. That's just practical. But in the first century, a small movement of Jesus had flourished. These new disciples of Jesus—many of whom had, until recently, participated in the pagan practices of Corinth—were awkwardly and clumsily sorting out their new way of life. At some point, someone asked, Hey, wait, is it, like, *bad* if we buy and eat this meat that was sacrificed to pagan gods? It had apparently become such a thing that the apostle Paul decided to address the issue in a letter, writing:

> Some people are still so accustomed to idols that
> when they eat sacrificial food they think of it as
> having been sacrificed to a god, and since their con-
> science is weak, it is defiled. But food does not
> bring us near to God; we are no worse if we do not
> eat, and no better if we do.
>
> Be careful, however, that the exercise of your rights
> does not become a stumbling block to the weak. For
> if someone with a weak conscience sees you, with
> all your knowledge, eating in an idol's temple,
> won't that person be emboldened to eat what is sac-
> rificed to idols? So this weak brother or sister, for
> whom Christ died, is destroyed by your knowledge.
> When you sin against them in this way and wound
> their weak conscience, you sin against Christ.
> Therefore, if what I eat causes my brother or sister
> to fall into sin, I will never eat meat again, so that I
> will not cause them to fall. (1 Corinthians 8v7-13)

To be fair, Paul isn't talking about art or entertainment, but his
logic has interesting ramifications well beyond the antiquated issue of idol meat. Second only to the Romans, "whatever is pure"
passage, 1 Corinthians 8v13 is easily among texts most invoked

against those of diverging taste in the arts. "If what I eat causes my brother or sister to fall into sin, I will never eat meat again." There you have it. Doesn't it logically follow that if what an artist creates or what an art enthusiast enjoys offends someone else, it should be forfeited for the sake of the offended party? There are a few problems with this line of thinking. If one presses Paul's original and hyper-specific context so far, Paul himself violates it. Even a small selection of Paul's writing would prove offensive to some Jewish readers, not to mention Gentiles, women, gay people, straight people, religious people, pagans, nonreligious people, married people, and eunuchs.

In Galatians, Paul is so frustrated with those who have made circumcision into a religious requirement that he says, "As for those agitators, I wish they would go the whole way and emasculate themselves!"[12] Scholars note that Paul may have intended a pun here. The Greek word he uses to describe "emasculation," more literally, means "cut off." So, Paul is saying, in his frustration, that he wishes these religious rule-mongers both be "cut off" from the community of God's people *and* cut off their own genitals. Double cut. That's pretty creative, Paul. Certainly, Paul's snappy wordplay for both excommunication and genital mutilation was probably offensive to some of his readers. I'd wager a guess that it remains offensive to many today. Is Paul breaking his own rule? Or is what Paul getting at more of a hyperbolic plea for the Corinthians to empathize with the new, ever-maturing believers of their own community? For Paul, there was nothing wrong with eating meat that was sacrificed to an idol, but remember, not every new disciple of Jesus in Corinth understood this just yet. So, he says, be considerate of them. Work it out together.

"Not offending" isn't an untenable ethic in which the sensibility of the other becomes the ultimate standard by which we may or may not create or receive art. When you follow that logic, you get problems with the entire Bible. So be considerate of one another. Work it out together.

ART: A REAL JOB

Regardless of how much or how little any given disciple of Jesus cares about art, they must accept and acknowledge that it matters deeply to God. Many disciples of Jesus have been uniquely gifted by God to create art, and many have been called by God to do so as their vocation. Not everyone will understand the artist's vocation nor the art they create, but that doesn't mean that the church shouldn't support them in their divine appointment. Rather than approach the artist's work with suspicion, it should be celebrated as having inherent value. After all, God himself is an artist. It is wrong to impose on artists any subjective moral standard based on individual sensibilities and ever-evolving cultural expectations. It is also wrong for a disciple of Jesus to disobey their Lord. No disciple of Jesus is to live in a self-contained bubble of individualism. The way of Jesus is always carried out in a community of shared life, mutual submission, and in self-sacrificial love.

Within the community of God's people, artists are to be encouraged, empowered, and released to do the work given them by God. The artist's vocation should be navigated with vulnerability, open to the accountability of other Christians and leaders. Like every aspect of the disciple's life, this work is to be honored as complex and multi-faceted. It may or may not fit basic expectations of what is pleasant or palatable, but God doesn't reduce art to such base standards, and neither should we.

ACT IV: BLASPHEMY, SEX, VIOLENCE, & PROFANITY

INTERMISSION

THE NEEDLES IN THE NECK

ON A MORNING 27 years after my friends broke my favorite record, I parked in the gravel lot of a tattoo shop and went inside. My friend and I made small talk as he readied his station. "Why this image in particular?" he asked, filling a small plastic cup with black ink.

How to answer? "It means a lot to me," I told him.

I lay flat on my back, turning my head all the way to my right shoulder as per his instructions. I took a long, sad breath when I heard the buzzing sound of the gun, like an angry hornet.

"This is going to suck," my friend reminded me. The hot, searing needles dug into the tender flesh of my neck. "Is it a fossil?" he asked me over the growl of the gun.

"No," I told him. "It's a millipede."

CHAPTER 4:1

SATANIC IN A GOOD WAY

I WAS SITTING IN a seminary class one afternoon when Robert Eggers's 2015 indie horror movie *The Witch* was mentioned. Rated R by the MPA for disturbing violent content and graphic nudity, *The Witch* depicts the demonic oppression of a farmer's family in 1630 New England. (This chapter contains massive spoilers for *The Witch*, by the way.) But *The Witch* made more headlines than usual for an indie flick when The Satanic Temple publicly endorsed the film. Writing in a statement: "As Satanists, we are ever mindful of the plight of women and outsiders throughout history who suffered under the hammer of theocracy and yet fought to empower themselves... Eggers' film… features a declaration of feminine independence that both provokes puritanical America and inspires a tradition of spiritual transgression."[1]

So why is an organization called The Satanic Temple so keen to endorse *The Witch*? Is it because the film celebrates the devil, encourages ritual sacrifice, and blasphemes God? No, apparently, it's because *The Witch* is "a declaration of feminine independence" and is "mindful of the plight of women and outsiders throughout history." Interestingly, just about anyone who knows a thing or two about the Bible would say that Jesus was as well. But when you put it like that, *The Witch* doesn't sound so bad. It doesn't sound "satanic" at all, actually. It sounds Christian. *The Witch* follows a sad, fundamentalist Puritan family so devoted to archaic religious thinking that they are banished from the New England settlement they called home and forced to make a new life at the edge of a dark forest. Things get worse when the family becomes oppressed by a sinister, spiritual evil lurking in the woods.

In my seminary class one afternoon, a discussion around discernment in art and entertainment was broached. I argued that generalizing blanket statements tend to do more harm than good. A friend of mine disagreed but struggled to cite the best example of a work of art he believed to be clearly and universally off-limits for all Christians. Finally, it occurred to him! I think we can all agree, he said, that no Christian has any business watching a piece of trash like *The Witch*. I replied immediately: *The Witch* was one of my favorite movies of 2015.

This friend of mine had never seen *The Witch*. He'd caught a trailer, maybe, or he'd heard about the infamous Satanic Temple endorsement. Why was he so disgusted at the very thought of *The Witch,* and why did I like it? It seems to me that both my classmate and the Satanic Temple were focusing on the surface while ignoring the substance. The movie, I'll admit, is certainly not for everyone. There's no graphic violence or gore, but the *implied* violence is worse. Much of the film's tension is built from the disappearance of the infant Samuel, who is stolen from his family and sacrificed by a witch. The family begins to devolve in despair. One evening, Samuel's mother, Katherine dreams Samuel has been miraculously returned to her. She cradles the baby in tearful maternal relief as she begins to nurse him by firelight in the peaceful quiet of their cottage. Then, the film abruptly cuts to a jarring wide shot of an enormous black raven violently pecking Katherine's bare breast as she cries out in agony and grief.

After a long and arduous descent into madness across the film's 92-minute runtime, the family's eldest daughter, Thomasin, eventually watches as their billy goat "Black Phillip," gores her father, William, to death. Before he dies, William, bleeding from his mouth, quotes from the book of Job: "Corruption, thou art my father."[2] The film concludes when the devil himself visits Thomasin, inviting her to sign over her soul as he purrs, "Wouldst thou live deliciously?" Thomasin, bloodied and naked, wanders into the forest to join a coven of cackling, levitating women as they shriek with laughter, floating into the night sky. Cut to black. As I watched this series of horrors unfold on the silver screen, I never understood the film's narrative as a celebration of anything it depicted. The movie draws from a toolbox of horror tropes to inform the viewer that what is happening is bad, not good. The color palette is cold and muted. The score is built from ominous strings and dissonant soundscapes. The tension is mounting and dreadful. During *The Witch*, the viewer is put in an awful predicament. Though you resent the heavy, patriarchal, religious fundamentalism with which William oppresses his family, you are made to empathize with his seemingly genuine struggle to protect them. Though you resent the cruel way Thomasin is falsely accused of witchcraft—and her subsequent estrangement from her family— you also don't want to see her family violently torn apart. The characters are human, broken, and sympathetic.

By the time the devil is finally revealed as the architect of the family's ruin, his deception is obvious. The devil doesn't come to liberate Thomasin from the bondage of religious oppression; he *exploits* religious oppression in order to destroy Thomasin and her family. The final moments of *The Witch* play as bleak and nihilistic (an enduring mainstay of the horror genre), not celebratory or triumphant.

Making the devil the hero of *The Witch* requires bizarre interpretive gymnastics. Less than ten minutes into the first act, a witch abducts a helpless infant and kills him. Next to die is a young boy named Caleb, who sets off in search of his lost baby brother. Eventually, Thomasin's often-cruel father and mentally unstable mother die as well, but not before the devil has engineered the murder of innocent children in an effective effort to lay waste to an entire family. To interpret *The Witch* as some kind of empowering triumph, you have to celebrate infanticide, child murder, and mental illness. If you think all of that is justifiable so a young woman can have some kind of devilish awakening, then yeah, I guess hail Satan. But I didn't see it that way. To me, *The Witch* was a harrowing and theologically astute fable depicting demonic oppression. It was clear to me that the viewer was not meant to interpret what was happening to young Thomasin and her family as a good thing.

So, I told my seminary class that *The Witch* did not incite me to sin, blaspheme, or lust. It did not numb me to the reality of demonic oppression—on the contrary, it was a poignant and affecting meditation on exactly that. It did not "open the door" for demonic influence; it was an invitation to slam it shut. God was on my mind throughout the entire film and afterward as I considered its images and ideas. My professor was also a bit reticent to condone watching horror movies about the devil, but later in the same conversation approved of at least one cinematic devil depiction. During *The Passion of the Christ's* relentless flogging sequence, the devil shows up. Depicted as an androgynous, strangely beautiful figure in a black coat, the devil moves amongst a crowd of onlookers cradling a baby. The camera moves in, and the viewer realizes something is amiss. Thick patches of dark hair cover the baby's back, and when it turns its head, it's not the face of a baby at all but a leering old man. When the "baby" beholds Jesus's misery, it smiles from ear to ear.

My professor—a Ph.D. who has taught classes on demons and the Bible all over the world for decades—was impressed by the sequence. "That's what Satan is like," he said. "He corrupts innocent things. He lies. He comes in the guise of something beautiful and sows corruption." I agreed. Quality interpretation, professor. But in the same conversation, this professor urged the class to abstain from movies like *The Witch, Evil Dead*, or *The Exorcist*. Why? As if on cue, someone in the class mentioned Philippians. "Is it *true*?" they asked. "Is it noble, right, pure, lovely, admirable, excellent and praiseworthy?"

"Yes," I said.

From where I sit, what *The Witch* has to say about spiritual evil and religious fundamentalism is true. The endeavor of creative artistry is noble and right. The emotional impact of the story and its images are lovely. The artistic craftsmanship is admirable, excellent. The feat of filmmaking is praiseworthy. What exactly makes *The Witch* a subject of debate? Because it's about the devil? The devil features throughout the Bible in vivid imagery, metaphor, and parables. He's depicted as a dragon, a lion, a sea monster, a snake. Why can't he be represented as a hairy man-baby? As a black goat? To the kind of alarmism that might argue *The Witch* could inspire genuine satanism, remember, once again, so does the Bible. In Satanism, the figure of the devil is used as a symbol of autonomy and rebellion against God. For Satanists, the devil is the ultimate figure of self-sufficiency. This image of Satan is lifted directly from the pages of Scripture. And it's not wrong. This is why Anton Lavey—author of *The Satanic Bible*—can read passages of the Bible and say, "Hey! This devil guy is really on to something!" While someone like me reads the same stories only to conclude: he's a liar.

Jex Blackmore, spokesperson for The Satanic Temple, thinks *The Witch* is "satanic" in a good way, and I agree. Only for me, "Satanic in a good way" means that the movie's handling of satanic ideas and imagery was appropriately unpleasant and accurately awful. Both of us really liked the movie. I was never tempted to understand *The Witch* as an actual guide to spiritual warfare; it was clearly a work of fiction. But I was also aware that this fiction was anchored in something that is, in my worldview, reality. After seeing *The Witch*, I found the Satanic Temple's endorsement hilariously ironic. *This* was the movie that their spokesperson called "a transformative Satanic experience that, in its call to arms, becomes an act of spiritual sabotage and liberation from the oppressive traditions of our forefathers"?[3] Huh.

The basic argument of the Satanic Temple is sensible enough: *The Witch* depicts the dangers of religious oppression, patriarchy, and the historical tendency to scapegoat innocent women as instruments of the devil to silence them. The movie's tone communicates all these things as *bad*. I agree. But the problem with the Satanic Temple's enthusiasm is that, in *The Witch*, the devil is an actual personal entity. In *The Witch*, witches are real. Supernatural evil is real. So, while Thomasin's family is disastrously mistaken in their fear that their daughter has become a witch, the devil *does* show up to manipulate this family and their religious fundamentalism so that everything is taken from Thomasin and her family is brought to violent disrepair—her family's misplaced paranoia becoming the catalyst that activates the thing they most feared.

But let's say that *The Witch is* deliberately satanic. So what? Do *we* become satanic for seeing it any more than we would for reading an interview with Jex Blackmore or reading the devil's dialogue with Jesus in the gospel of Matthew? Isn't that same dialogue, understood by one audience, celebrating Satan while another interprets it to condemn him?

In his memoir *The Pastor*, Eugene Peterson recalls a fascinating incident in which a church janitor asked to paint his portrait. When Peterson beheld the finished project, he was surprised. "He had painted me in a black pulpit robe, seated with a red Bible on my lap, my hands folded over it. The face was gaunt and grim, the eyes flat and without expression."[4] The artist told Peterson, "[I painted you] as you would look in 20 years if you insisted on being a pastor… Eugene, the church is an evil place. No matter how good you are and how good your intentions, the church will suck the soul out of you. I'm your friend. Please, don't be a pastor."[5]

This artist used a painting to symbolically condemn both the church and the call of God over Eugene Peterson's life. Certainly, one might describe a work of art intended by the artist to condemn the church and to dissuade a man appointed by God to become a pastor as satanic. But what did Peterson do with this satanic painting? He kept it. Even called it *prophetic*. "His prophetic portrait entered my imagination and has never faded out. But I didn't follow his counsel. Eventually I did become a pastor. But I have also kept that portrait in a closet in my study for 55 years as a warning: Willi's prophecy of the desolation that he was convinced the church would visit on me if I became a pastor. I still pull it out occasionally and look at those vacant eyes, flat and empty. The face gaunt and unhealthy. Willi's artistic imagination created a portrait that was far more vivid than any verbal warning."[6] The artist intended the painting to condemn and prevent Eugene Peterson's work as a pastor, but Eugene Peterson interpreted it as an encouragement. What's funny about me arguing here, on the page, with The Satanic Temple's interpretation of an indie horror movie, is that Robert Eggers, the guy who wrote and directed *The Witch,* is adamant he had no ideological statement in mind with *The Witch* one way or the other. "I don't say, 'This is an idea that I am thinking about, that I want to explore using the past'—I don't do it like that. Often, it's just a series of images and an atmosphere that is compelling to me, and then in doing my research, the story emerges."[7] So, the guy who *made* the thing doesn't seem to agree with The Satanic Temple *or* me. Go figure. This means, among other things, that neither one of us is "right" in the exact sense. And to be fair, Jex Blackmore isn't even here to comment.

CHAPTER 4:2

SEX, PORN, AND RADIOLOGY TECHNICIANS

LET'S IMAGINE A RADIOLOGY technician who follows Jesus. Surely, they exist, but ours is hypothetical. For the sake of this exercise, let's imagine this technician is a man who is attracted to women. He is passionate about his work as a radiology technician and feels appointed by God to do it. He follows his calling, applies his education, works hard, and does his job well. His job requires that he assist with routine mammograms. Now, let's imagine a hypothetical workday in the life of our theoretical rad tech.

A woman enters. Our imaginary technician, though he is professional and of sound integrity, finds the woman very attractive. The job at hand is a mammogram. The technician must usher this topless woman to a machine where he will help position her breasts for a series of pictures. Is this disciple of Jesus in an inherently compromising position? His vocation, his job, his passion all place this man in a position that requires him to see and to even touch naked women. Regardless of his integrity and professionalism, as a human being, he may inevitably find some of these women physically attractive. I venture a guess that most readers will agree that there is nothing inherently wrong with this man's vocation. On the contrary, many readers will likely think it an admirable and worthwhile gig. Sure, our theoretical rad tech could sin by objectifying the women he encounters in his line of work, but we invite this person to integrity in navigating these situations without asking them to abandon their calling because the world needs radiology technicians. With doctors, we similarly grant that theirs is good and necessary work. So, we opt to trust their maturity and professionalism to the degree that they can interact with the human body without necessarily objectifying or abusing their position or their patients. We grant that some do, but we concede that a doctor's role in society is too crucial to forfeit based on the possibility of misuse. But for artists and art lovers, the church rarely grants such confidence.

There are several analogies we could take in similar directions. Sex therapists, OBGYNs, personal trainers, and yoga instructors, to name a few, operate in fields that intersect with sexuality and the human body. For the most part, disciples of Jesus acknowledge and respect the validity of vocations like these, but many seem to imply that while a job like practicing medicine is valid and necessary, art is not.

Why? Why is it not valid and worthwhile for an artist to explore and address human sexuality and physicality in ways that help us understand, celebrate, and acknowledge what God has made good about both and how they can be, tragically, abused? We understand that doctors can see and touch bodies without doing harm to themselves and their patients. Therapists can discuss the sexual exploits of their patients without fantasizing about them. Personal trainers can work intimately with the physicality of their clients without objectifying them. But for many, the idea that an artist can interact with, address, or depict sexuality without sinning—or that other disciples of Jesus can experience and appreciate that art without sinning—is inconceivable.

It's not exactly a new idea. Michelangelo's work inside the Sistine Chapel provoked the ire of delicate sensibilities for years. One journalist wrote, "It was called a 'sin,' a 'stew of nudes' that could 'weaken the faith of others.'… a torrent of complaints about the works' rampant, joyful nudity rocked the global Catholic Church."[1] Art historian Elizabeth Lev observed that Michelangelo seems to have commented on his critics through subsequent additions to the painting. The papal courtier Biagio da Cesena had denounced the painting, calling it "disgraceful that in so sacred a place there should have been depicted all those nude figures, exposing themselves so shamefully." In response, Cesena was worked into the piece as judge of the underworld. He has donkey ears (to indicate foolishness), and a snake is devouring his genitals. Lev argued, "What Michelangelo was proposing is that if you look at this painting and all you can see are naked bodies, and all you can see is pornography, the problem is you, not me."[2] Centuries after Cesena was so affronted by the Sistine Chapel, author and pastor John Piper revived Cesena's critique of Michelangelo's work. "I come away with the serious question whether all these ubiquitous private parts are a devout message, or a subtle disdain for the church. Is the in-your-face exposure of God's buttocks really a faithful exposition of Exodus 33v23? Or is the pope being mooned?"[3]

Sex and the human body have always been important subjects in the arts (including the creative prose of the Bible), dating all the way back to the creation of human beings, who were created naked and without shame. God opted to include extended passages of erotic poetry in the Bible in which the author celebrates his lover's breasts,[4] and she, in turn, sure seems to extol the pleasures of performing oral sex on him.[5] These artistic and sexually explicit passages are most certainly included in the Bible for us to read. Naked human bodies are good, but our experience of them is painfully subject to a world broken and bent out of shape by sin. What should be beautiful often becomes mishappened by objectification and abuse.

Who is the arbiter of what qualifies as the type of sexuality one cannot enjoy without sinning? What makes a person objectify others? If the Genesis story inspires imaginative images of a nude Adam and Eve, is this wrong to paint or to see? What about a beautiful painting of two nude lovers intended to celebrate marital bliss inspired by Song of Songs? Would such a thing be wrong to create or to display? Does the image become sinful to behold if it moves—a film rather than a painting? What if the painting was subtle, but a description of the painting was graphic? Would the visuals be more sinful than the words describing them?

How we answer these questions will differ wildly from person to person because few people experience sexual desire in exactly the same way. Each disciple of Jesus must exercise wise discernment and seek both the Holy Spirit and the accountability of the church in navigating the grey area.

GOOD SEX, BAD SEX

In 2019, Dan Reed's shocking documentary *Leaving Neverland* generated overwhelming controversy across the world. In it, two men detail allegations that pop star Michael Jackson had sexually abused them as children. The documentary opened a larger cultural conversation around the methods of sexual predators and how further abuse can be stopped or prevented. The documentary is well-made and effective, and its descriptions of child molestation are easily among the most sexually explicit and disturbing I've ever experienced in any film. A pedophile, however, may find them arousing. But what if Dan Reed had not been a documentary filmmaker? What if the same story struck him, and with the same purpose and motivation, he had instead translated that inspiration into a fictionalized narrative, say, a movie. Or a novel. The same story inspiring it, the same motivation to expose and combat sexual abuse, but through a medium more abstracted from the source.

Would such a movie or book inspire a different kind of outrage? Would the same audience endure it? Defend it? Appreciate it?

David Fincher's adaptation of *The Girl with the Dragon Tattoo* features several scenes of graphic sexual assault and rape. The novel on which the film is based begins with the epigraph: "Eighteen percent of the women in Sweden have at one time been threatened by a man."[6] It is abundantly clear in their handling of the issue that both the novel and the film mean to denounce, not celebrate, the sexual violence depicted on the page and on the screen. For many readers and viewers, these scenes are overwhelming. But isn't this the point? Not titillation, but an exposé of often overlooked violence against women in order to condemn it.

I know a couple that worked out an arrangement for deciding which movies they would and would not watch together. One member of this couple was convinced that it was impossible for men to see images of sex and nudity without lusting. She would screen certain movies and shows prior to her husband to decide whether they were appropriate for him.

What about you? I asked.

What do you mean?

What if *you* lust?

Oh, that stuff doesn't affect me, she said.

She was arguing that it is entirely possible for someone to experience certain depictions of sexuality without sinning. In this case, she had decided that it was impossible for men, but not for women, to escape sexuality in art unscathed. This is a popular opinion, but it isn't true. One 2018 study published by the National Library of Medicine found that more than 60% of women reported consuming pornography within the month they were surveyed.[7] Many movies that include nudity and sexuality do so with intentions that exclude "entertainment" or titillation. Even so, some of those same movies could make a particular person lust, and some may not. Some men find dressed women more arousing than undressed women. Some women find depictions of emotional affairs more arousing than gratuitous sex scenes. If your black-and-white rubric accounts for only "naked people having sex," you ironically leave little room for the kind of nuanced discernment necessary to protect one's soul from art that features neither thing but that could still provoke one to lust. In the end, a healthy understanding of sexuality in art will likely frustrate those in want of black-and-white boundaries.

PORN IS NOT ART

Let's get this one out of the way. Porn is not art. That's an easy one. Though the notion is debated amongst art theorists and pornographers (big surprise), it is settled easily for the disciple of Jesus. Pornography is intrinsically exploitative and always harmful. Art is not. Pornography is an inherently and fundamentally irredeemable cesspool of evil—an entire industry built on the exploitation and abuse of human beings, the psychological enslavement of its consumers, and human trafficking of its "performers." To consume pornography is to condone, support, and further the abuse, violence, and enslavement of human beings made in God's image.

Philosopher Alva Noë argues that the one-dimensional purpose of pornography immediately disqualifies it as art. Porn, by definition, is an instrument for sexual arousal. This is the singular function of porn. But art, Noë says, subverts function. Art can be functional or functionless. Art can evoke wildly varied—even opposing—reactions from one spectator to the next. Porn is always and only a harmful instrument of exploitative sexual objectification. If porn does not titillate, it fails, as this is its only function or purpose. Art *can* be exploitative, but not necessarily. More complicated still, porn is never art, but art sometimes includes porn.

Bret Easton Ellis's controversial novel *American Psycho* is overwhelmingly gratuitous in every conceivable way. Purposefully loathsome narrator Patrick Bateman blathers on about his outfits, exercise routines, dinner plans, and his sexual exploits with prostitutes, not to mention the rape, torture, and mutilation of many of the same women. The sexual passages in *American Psycho* are pornographic, but like it or not, *American Psycho* is art. That doesn't mean you have to like it or approve of its techniques. It just means it is what it is. The porn in the novel is not art, but the novel itself is.

Novelist Irvine Welsh wrote about the porn prose in *American Psycho*, saying, "The objective of pornography is to produce sexual arousal. While *American Psycho* includes pornographic scenes, they are carefully crafted and placed, and juxtaposed with horror and gore. They are not about a twisted writer's deviant projections, engineered to fuel the misogynistic fantasies of a (hopefully small) contingent of dysfunctional male readers. In those scenes, I see only a technician at work, albeit one operating in tandem with a monstrous character he has forged as the (appropriate) tool to guide his story and address his themes."[8] *American Psycho* uses pornography to satirize excess, and in doing so, critiques and condemns the excess of pornography. For more than three decades, the novel has enjoyed (or suffered) an infamous legacy for its particular approach to satire. When reading the book, I could turn a page and behold from afar an outpouring of sexual depravity and gather, Ah, here's another sex scene. My personal preference was to skip ahead. Though anyone is free to disagree, I think Welsh got it right. I didn't care for the porn passages, nor did I read them, but they seemed to me a creative decision that suited the author's purpose: To mercilessly skewer a world of superficiality so devoid of humanity that everything is objectified, consumed, destroyed. In this sense, the inclusion of pornography became a mockery of it.

A peer of Ellis, Chuck Palahniuk, did a similar thing with his novel *Snuff*. Spectacularly nauseating, *Snuff* details the inner workings of the porn industry as its protagonist plans to die during the filming of one of her adult movies. Nothing in *Snuff* glamorizes pornography in any way. It repulses. What Upton Sinclair's novel *The Jungle* said of the meat industry, Palahniuk's *Snuff* says of the porn industry. These are extreme examples, and I would never recommend *American Psycho* or *Snuff* to the average reader. I don't like or dislike these author's methods, per se, but I think I understand them as tools.

Most of the time, we aren't talking about cases this complicated or over-the-top. Recently, a friend of mine expressed interest in seeing the latest in a long line of *A Star is Born* remakes. He asked if the movie was good, and someone among us said it was. My friend, the one who'd asked in the first place, hesitated to accept this assessment, saying, I heard it was porn. By that, he meant that in one scene, a woman's breasts are partially exposed. The scene was so incidental, so peripheral that I couldn't remember it being in the movie at all. I honestly couldn't imagine being compelled to lust by this kind of blink-and-you'll-miss-it semi-nudity, but I do acknowledge and respect that another disciple of Jesus is well within their rights to abstain from the film if they do not trust themselves to honor the actor in question without objectifying them. It's not the movie's problem, not the actor's issue, it's the viewer's. Like Jesus said, if your right eye causes you to sin, gouge it out. I also expect this kind of communal courtesy to run both ways.

WISDOM AND NAKED PEOPLE

The actual consideration here in navigating sexuality in art is not "Are there naked people?" or "Does it depict sex?" Once again, the way forward is with wise discernment. Informed by the Holy Spirit and worked out in the community of God's people. In the same way that we understand and acknowledge our imaginary radiology technician's ability to perform a mammogram without sinning, we carry that same logic into our understanding of art. Not all sexually explicit art incites lust, and what does incite lust for one may not for another. We evaluate our reactions and temptations with discernment, submitted to the authority of Jesus and to the accountability of Christian community. We ask God about it. We talk to the people with whom we share life, making room for vulnerability. And we begin with these core values in place: Sex is good. So is art.

CHAPTER 4:3

ON CUSSING

TOOTH & NAIL RECORDS was, in the early 90s, perhaps the first noteworthy outlet for Christian bands and musicians with no interest and no place in the American Christian Music Machine. Tooth & Nail worked with professing Christians, yes, but to make (of all things) good music. Not a sanitized spiritual product for Christian Bookstore consumption, but art.

One of Tooth & Nail's more alienating acts was an abrasive punk band called Ninety Pound Wuss. Disbanding Christian commerce cynicism and tour fatigue, members of Ninety Pound Wuss went on to form the controversial Seattle act Raft of Dead Monkeys, whose debut EP, *D.B.M.,* featured profanity-laden lyrics about violence and terrorism. Fans of Ninety Pound Wuss assumed the band had gone the way of apostasy. It was likely, they assumed, the same tired story of post-evangelical Christians who had bailed out on the church were now spreading their newly secularized wings. But some of the Raft of Dead Monkey's founders and songwriters still claimed to follow Jesus. They were involved in local churches. Some of them were pastors. Raft of Dead Monkeys was, apparently, a satire. A band designed as a performance art experiment in parodying religious and political extremism. From even a cursory glance, the whole thing was absurd and over the top. It seemed obvious that the Raft of Dead Monkeys schtick wasn't meant to be taken at face value. But people were still upset, and the few people paying attention were *most* upset about all the *cussing.*

I sometimes like cuss words, but I don't ever use them, personally. I really don't. Ask my friends. I grew up in a household where cussing did not occur. I wasn't oblivious to swearing. I went to public school. All my friends from junior high and upward populated their vocabularies with copious amounts of bad words. In the eighties and early nineties, even family movies were laced with profanity. I learned the F-word in 1988 when I saw *Beetlejuice,* which was rated PG. I knew all the swears, understood (almost) all of them, and didn't really mind them. I just never used them. Today, the alleged "sinfulness" of certain words, in and of themselves, is an area of disagreement. As I pointed out earlier, there are at least a couple of instances in the Bible of what would, in context, probably qualify as "cussing." Depending on which scholar you're reading, there might be more. But in any event, each of them requires translation and context for us to understand them as swears.

Cussing changes over time, from culture to culture and language to language. In her delightful volume *On Cussing*, Katherine Dunn notes, "It's interesting to me that all during the medieval millennium, when blasphemy was so shocking, the words and subjects that we now consider quite obscene, or at least rude, were perfectly ordinary in polite conversation."[9] Any American who ventures to Europe or Australia learns that we grade the severity of cuss words differently. In my family growing up, saying "butt" was offensive, but "booty" or "hiney" was fine. "Poot" was a necessary proxy for the ultra-taboo "fart."

Any given word, in and of itself, is unremarkable. They are characters on a page or sounds from someone's mouth. I know people who swear in languages they don't speak (Scheisse!), because "the real thing" feels too crass. But in a different language? The word is virtually nonsense. We, as societies, imbue words with power and then wield them for good or for evil. Case in point, in Jesus's famous manifesto, the sermon on the mount, he warns against calling people stupid. "But I tell you that anyone who is angry with a brother or sister will be subject to judgment. Again, anyone who says to a brother or sister, 'Raca,' is answerable to the court. And anyone who says, 'You fool!' will be in danger of the fire of hell." (Matthew 5v22.) The word Jesus mentions, *raca*, is an Aramaic expression of contempt—something like calling someone "empty-headed." The second term, "you fool," is not unlike the first. Both were common, everyday utterances, equally employed, equally severe. If you were in Jesus's audience, you might have chuckled at the idea of someone being taken to court for uttering an ordinary, seemingly insignificant slight. Jesus's punch line comes as an unexpected jolt. If you think it absurd to be prosecuted over calling someone dumb, I'm telling you that you are even in danger of *the fire of hell*.

That word that most of our Bibles translate as *hell* is *Gehenna*—a well-known physical location outside of Jerusalem, also called the valley of Hinnom. Gehenna was a detestable site of human sacrifice by fire to the pagan god Molech. It later became something like a landfill where the city's waste was thrown and burned. Gehenna's reputation was so vivid that Jesus often used it as an analogy to describe the final destruction of the wicked. This passage in Matthew is one such example. Jesus was saying, Listen, the kind of anger that compels a person to call a brother or sister stupid is as severe as a crime. In fact, calling a brother or sister a fool is so severe it could land you in the city dump to be discarded and, in the final judgment, destroyed.

Two things are clear enough in this teaching. First, words matter. But what matters even more is the emotional disposition out of which words flow. This premise often occurs in the teaching of Jesus. Some argue, only the heart matters, not the words. Say whatever you want as long as you're not mean! But this logic breaks down. In discipleship to Jesus, concern for the other typically supersedes the freedom of the individual. Meaning, in the technical sense, swear words themselves aren't really "sinful," so much as the angry, vindictive, or crass sentiment that gives them locomotion. Anyone who has heard a considerable amount of swearing understands that people often swear without being angry, vindictive, or crass. But the disposition of the cussing party is only one piece of a two-part equation. The other, more important question is: How do the people in my life experience the words I say?

Of course, one can stretch this logic to its breaking point. Like Paul's assessment of meat sacrificed to idols, consideration for others in language can't apply to all of humanity all the time, or even Jesus violates his own teaching. But really, when it comes to offensive language in art, this conversation takes a turn.

WHEN FICTIONAL CHARACTERS CUSS

Let's start here: I don't use swear words, personally. I do, however, sometimes write stories in which characters use swear words. Why? As an author, I sometimes create characters that say and do things I may or may not approve of or agree with.

My wife isn't particularly bothered by swearing, but when we watched Kevin Phillips's excellent thriller *Super Dark Times*, the amount of cussing became, for her, obnoxious. In the film, a group of small-town teenage boys swear profusely. Like Holden

Caulfield in *The Catcher in the Rye*, they seem, like many teenagers, posturing and insecure. They discuss sex and masturbation, being aroused by Jamie Lee Curtis in *True Lies*, smoking weed.

Good grief, my wife said during one of these scenes of dialogue. Are there really teenage boys like this?

Yes, I said. Absolutely. The performances and dialogue rang so true to my experience that they sounded like anything I might have overheard on a school bus or walking to class. It was what we might call an honest use of swearing in art.

Stephen King put it wonderfully in his advice to write realistic characters that may very well cuss. "The Legion of Decency might not like the word *shit*, and you might not like it much either, but sometimes you're stuck with it."[10] When my children were very small, I didn't show them movies or play them songs loaded with swearing. Not because I think the words themselves are somehow dangerous to hear, but because they're not quite old enough to understand the divisive and destructive power of certain words. Eventually and inevitably, my kids will probably learn all the swears, and as they do, I will do my best to teach them why we do and do not use certain words, why their mom and dad don't use certain words, and why characters in movies and books sometimes do.

The ability to shock or offend an audience is a useful communicative tool at an artist's disposal. Katherine Dunn writes, "A writer's aim should be to give genuine thought to the use of this limited but significant vocabulary [of cuss words], and above all to avoid cliché and tedium."[11] You don't have to like or even approve of swearing to understand its validity in a work of art. An artistic depiction of a thing is not an artist's approval of a thing, and even if an artist *does* approve of a thing they depict, it doesn't mean the audience must do likewise.

If disciples of Jesus practice consideration for others, they will constantly work to corral the dangerous power of their own words. Art is one of the ways we can grapple with and process this. A book like *The Catcher in the Rye* or a film like *Super Dark Times* offers insight into the way language belies insecurity. A band like Raft of Dead Monkeys gives us space to explore the outrageousness of language.

But I wouldn't play it for my kids. Yet.

CHAPTER 4:4

VIOLENCE BEGETS VIOLENCE

WHEN STEVEN SPIELBERG RELEASED his epic war drama *Saving Private Ryan* in 1998, everyone was talking about the *violence.* For upwards of twenty minutes, viewers are plunged into the hellish world of Omaha Beach on June 6, 1944. The body count is staggering. The tide literally runs red with blood. The movie was met with near-unanimous acclaim and is widely regarded as one of the greatest films ever made. Janet Maslin of *The New York Times* called *Saving Private Ryan* "the finest war movie of our time."[1] When people talk about *Saving Private Ryan*, they almost always mention its brutality, citing it as a benchmark for realism in mainstream cinema. Would *Saving Private Ryan* have had such a profound impact and enjoy such a lasting legacy had it been less brutal? I doubt it.

Brian De Palma—the director behind movies like *Carrie* and *Scarface*—was once asked if the violence in his films was included proudly. He answered, "It's not a question of proudly or not proudly. Violence is justified in certain movies. The level of violence in something like *Saving Private Ryan* makes sense because Spielberg is trying to show something about the brutality of what happened. I think in 'Scarface' the violence was warranted; what I showed on the screen was nothing compared to what's happening on the news every night, where they find people cut up in garbage dumpsters."[2]

An artist might depict violence for the sake of creating something consistent with reality, but violence in art can be about more than accuracy. Psychologist Glenn Walters argues that three factors likely attract viewers to violent horror films.[3] The first is the tension generated by being frightened or shocked. The second is relevance (either personally or culturally)—the idea that "this could actually happen" or the pressing question of "what would I do if it did?" But Walters' final factor was *unrealism*. People are attracted to the horror, violence, and morbidity of certain films because it isn't real. In this exchange, the viewer enjoys the safety of the gallery during the surgery. They are not on the table.

Violence is an inescapable reality of our world. Humans can be drawn to violence, prone to it, averse to it, afraid of it, predisposed to it, exposed to it, immersed in it. We are perpetrators of violence or victimized by it or both. Violence shocks and appalls, and yet we are simultaneously curious about and afraid of it. Our reaction to violence is visceral and can manifest in a broad emotional spectrum: Outrage and disgust (viral videos of beheadings carried out by terrorist groups), panic and despair (a fatal car accident), fear and anxiety (a slasher movie), excitement and adrenaline (first-person shooter video games), extreme distress (child abuse), or even humor (*Jackass* or *The Itchy & Scratchy Show*). In other words, it's hard to imagine a concept *more* fitting for artistic exploration. Art can provide an appropriate venue for us to process the reality of violence. Violence in art and fiction explores that which is often beyond our experience, like the depiction of wealth or travel or vigilantism—we can imagine and consider that which is alien to us.

When artists utilize violent imagery to entertain rather than repel us, they allow us to confront our innate fears and survive, like riding a rollercoaster. But this is a complicated idea for the disciple of Jesus. Because Jesus teaches nonviolence and enemy love. For hundreds of years, there was unanimous agreement within the Christian movement that it is never appropriate for a disciple of Jesus to use violence against another person under any circumstances. No violent self-defense, no violence against state enemies, no violence ever. Today, the issue of Christian nonviolence is debated, but this isn't a book about nonviolence.[4] At the very least, all disciples of Jesus must agree that violence is tragic, regrettable, and well outside of God's ideal and design for human flourishing. So, how should Christians understand violence in art?

I am a pacifist. I have written and taught extensively on the subject of Christian nonviolence. As a novelist and lyricist, I find violence a particularly compelling issue. Sometimes, people ask me, "How can a pacifist include such violent imagery in their art?" Of course, this question presupposes that an artistic depiction of a thing is an artist's endorsement of a thing. As if *Saving Private Ryan* was a celebration of the tragic loss of life during World War II. The idea that a pacifist would value the aesthetics of violence makes sense. How else can one communicate the horror of violence—the wrongness of it—than to depict it as horrible and wrong? As author Philip Graham Ryken said so well, "God can use transgressive art to awaken the conscience and arouse a desire for a better world."[5]

But that doesn't mean that any artist depicting something violent must have some overt, explicit moral agenda in mind. I think it can be appropriate to use violence in art for the sake of thrilling an audience. Some people seem to believe that when one enjoys something like *Rambo III* or *Dawn of the Dead,* they do so with a kind of sick, sadistic pleasure. Violence porn. But I think that many (if not most) people who read *Gone Girl* or watch *Kill Bill* aren't sadists or sociopaths. Instead, we're curious. Art allows us to confront violence without experiencing it or being overcome by it. Art enables us to mock violence, face death, and address the ever-present specter of our mortality with a smirk rather than a scream. To relax. One film enables us to grapple with the horror of violence, while another allows us to release our fear of it, if only for a bit. Even as a pacifist, I like *Rambo III*. I like it as fiction, a story. I like the cinematic spectacle of it. But not all violence in art is spectacular.

The Omaha Beach sequence in *Saving Private Ryan* isn't "thrilling" in the traditional sense. It's harrowing, wholly unpleasant. The violence isn't funny or glamorous. It plays with a kind of cinematic realism. The impact is undeniable. Watching it reminds us of the real-life horror of war, generates empathy, comments on humanity and society, teaches us something. The same is true of works like William Golding's *The Lord of the Flies* or Alice Walker's *The Color Purple*. The violence in Stephen King's *The Stand,* however, or Tobe Hooper's *The Texas Chain Saw Massacre* is designed to shock and terrify. The violence in Peter Jackson's *Dead Alive* is designed to make us laugh and squirm. The violence in *John Wick* is designed to make us thrill and applaud. Art allows us to probe the emotional reservoirs of the human psyche and explore what makes us afraid, upset, or excited. We often emerge thinking, asking questions, having conversations.

There is inarguably more combat and death in a given Marvel Studios epic than in the average home invasion horror movie. One shocks and alienates us, the other excites and entertains us. Why? Because the aesthetics on the filmmaker's palette are utilized appropriately. Art is a vehicle for telling stories, exploring images, ideas, emotions. Of course, art can be irresponsible or tasteless in dealing with complex subjects like violence, and thus, we exercise discernment in what we choose to watch or read or see. Not everyone wants to read *The Stand* or watch *The Texas Chain Saw Massacre*, and that's fine. But even those with a strong, concrete moral aversion to violence can learn to understand why someone else might like slasher movies.

CODA: THE SHAPE OF ART TO COME

CODA

TOWARD A CHRISTIAN APPRECIATION OF ART

ART APPRECIATION—LIKE ANY other spiritual discipline—must be practiced. Every spiritual discipline—whether it's prayer, reading the Scriptures, or fasting—all of them come naturally to some and prove massively challenging for others. If prayer has been challenging in your apprenticeship to Jesus, that doesn't mean that prayer is less essential to your spiritual formation. If you happen to love reading the Bible, it doesn't mean that you can take it for granted. Art appreciation is not for creatives, film buffs, and music geeks only—God has invited all of us into an experience and appreciation of art and creativity. Like all the spiritual disciplines, art appreciation is a means to an end, and the end is God.

A healthy diet of art is crucial for learning to understand and appreciate the Bible. Many a fiery fundamentalist terrified of art has also understood the Bible as a completely literal, linear, moral encyclopedia. Unable to grasp its use of metaphor, hyperbole, and symbolism, they deform the world's most sophisticated work of literary genius into black and white guide to life in the modern world. If you scoff at the value and purpose of an abstract painting or an experimental novel, you are in big trouble when it comes to the Bible. Disciples of Jesus should read literary fiction, whether they consider themselves the reading type or not. They should read it as much as they read theology. Most of the Bible is narrative, and it can be mystifying, layered, offensive, complex. How will you learn to appreciate the genre the Bible most prefers if you do not steep yourself in that genre on a regular basis?

The benefits of art appreciation bleed into other avenues of spiritual formation, just as fasting from food fortifies the will and teaches us discipline in other areas of life. Prayer teaches us peace and patience in the ordinary rhythms of the day. Some gravitate to the arts naturally, but we're chaotic and undisciplined in our consumption of it. Others rarely, if ever, move beyond our very niche preferences. Some don't care for art at all, at least not on purpose. But all of us can learn rhythm and discipline in our appreciation of art. We can plan how many novels we will read in a year, make a schedule, keep it. We can teach ourselves to consider genres and mediums ordinarily lost on us. The first time I took my family to an art museum, I had little grasp on what we were looking at, to which style it belonged, by whom it was influenced, but I made an effort to slow down and look, and that's starting somewhere.

Each of the following three suggestions assumes we have decided to take art seriously and create rhythms and routines to accommodate art appreciation. Then, it begins with an investment.

THE INVESTMENT

The last few years have seen a veritable *mountain* of writing on the topic of our over-stimulated, over-busy, digitally addicted modern dystopian wasteland—both inside and outside of the church. You don't have to be a sociologist to see the writing on the wall. Every second of the day, we are bombarded with screens, entertainment dopamine, shopping possibilities, social media outrage, vitriol, and image curation. As the destructive Babylonian beast of digital horror devours everything in its path, the way we experience art has changed entirely.

When I was a teenager, I sometimes caught wind of new music through a friend, on the radio, or playing late-night on MTV. Often, this exposure would be little more than a single song (or a small selection of a single song). If I liked what I heard, I would devise some way to pool fifteen bucks (odd jobs, allowance, birthdays, whatever). Now, all I needed was a 45-minute ride into the city, where I could peruse a few record stores hoping to find the album that contained that interesting song I'd heard. If they didn't have it, they could order it for me, a process which involved filling out some paperwork and waiting for about six weeks. Then, eventually, that new music was mine. Easy breezy.

Sometimes, all this work paid off, and the album was immediately fantastic, but that was rare. More often, the album didn't reveal an obvious excellence upon first listen. But by then, I'd done all this work, hunted the dang thing down, so by God, I was going to work on liking it. And weirdly, I'd often come around on listen number eight or nine or twenty and learn to see things I missed.

To my estimation, the greatest, most enduring albums rarely jump out of your car stereo and announce, "This is the best!" The albums that seem to do this tend to fade. To really hear and see everything going on, more often than not, takes a decent amount of investment. This idea of investment applies to any and every work of art—the deliberate, disciplined decision to assign value to something rather than treating it as expendable fodder for consumption. Assigning value to a work of art doesn't mean you pretend to like everything or that to truly invest in a piece, you must somehow force yourself to love it. Assigning value to art means treating it as something more than disposable entertainment rolling down an avalanche of infinite options. Assigning value to art means giving it emotional and intellectual attention.

Our current models for entertainment are designed to reduce investment as much as possible. Scrolling absently through streaming services, our attention divided, eyes darting to our smartphones, we don't really care about taking a closer look at the work into which artists have poured themselves because we've invested nothing to consume it. Art has become free peanuts on the table, something to be chewed absently if at all, empty calories, take it or leave it. This means the lost art of investment is an upstream effort. We must go out of our way to seek out and embrace modes of investment that make the entire process ask more of us and take longer. This is good and good for us, and there are lots of ways to do it. All of them involve slowing down, giving greater time and attention to fewer things rather than a cursory glance or casual enjoyment of many things. So, turn your phone off before the movie begins. Sit through an album's entire runtime wearing headphones, doing nothing else. Read novels rather than listening to them on commutes. Something. Anything. Invest.

THE DISCUSSION

A big part of how we experience and understand art is in the way we discuss it with other humans. In the modern landscape of digital dystopia and sociopolitical outrage obsession, we typically either dismiss art like the cardboard that once housed a Happy Meal or fretfully refrain from any critique at all for fear of offending fragile social media sensibilities. But for as long as humans have made art, they've argued about what it means, if it's any good, and how it should be enjoyed and understood. There are ways to do this without being rude or arrogant or mean-spirited. I argue with my friends about movies so often and at such length that I eventually began hosting a podcast for exactly that reason. I can't count how often I've charged into a debate, guns blazing, to have someone across the table thoughtfully dismantle my critique in such a way that I staggered backward, collected myself, and saw the entire movie differently. I once changed a friend's opinion of the film *Whiplash* over a sandwich when I offered a different interpretation of the film's ending.

Few things enable us to better understand, appreciate, and approach different types of art than discussing them with other people. It's why we have book clubs and critics. It's why we go have dinner after the movie and talk about what it all means. A great indication of maturity is our ability to entertain other people's opinions without any felt need to adjust, insult, or dismiss them, *or* to adjust our own opinions in light of theirs. Other people's opinions—even ones we don't like, even ones we find immoral or repugnant—can often teach us a thing or two. Part of growing in emotional health and spiritual maturity means developing the disciplined wherewithal to stand on a secure foundation of your own faith and ideas and remain capable of grappling with new and divergent views without losing your footing. The discussion of art becomes a pan we use to sift through these ideas, looking for bits of truth or resonance—however small or abstract—and, with respect, letting that which is not true wash away without freaking the heck out about it.

The New Testament *assumes* all disciples of Jesus will work out their apprenticeship to Jesus and their spiritual formation in the dynamic give and take of community—the church. This is where we practice the spiritual discipline of art appreciation as well. The way we experience art is often very personal, but the Bible has no paradigm whatsoever for discipleship within Western individualism. *All* of life, for Christians, is set on the shared and imperfect table of life in community. So ask the art lovers in your life what they think about a given piece and talk about it. Be willing to learn from the perspectives of people with different tastes and fewer creative credentials. Our experience of art must be brought into the conversational accountability of the church, whether we're shy or gregarious, enthusiastic film buffs, or insecure and ignorant in the ways of critique.

DISCERNMENT & CONVICTION

These terms permeate this book like a chorus: wisdom, discernment, community. I believe that God's Spirit communicates with disciples of Jesus.[1] One genre of said communication is something called *conviction*. In simplest terms, conviction is a sensation given by God, the Bible, another person, or by one's own wisdom and common sense that something isn't right. This could come as a kind of mental or emotional uneasiness, a sudden realization, or through a series of phrases, images, or Scriptures that suddenly surface in the imagination by direct deposit of the Holy Spirit.

Tapping into this resource—readily available to all disciples of Jesus—and bringing that conviction into the accountability of church life, we can learn to operate in wise discernment while enjoying the arts. Here's an anecdote from my own life. I love the prophetic genius of the science fiction series *Black Mirror*. More of an anthology of short films than a TV series, *Black Mirror* is a dark and *very* bleak meditation on the direction our technology-addicted is headed. It's well-written, fascinating, upsetting, and obscene. None of *Black Mirror*'s particular brand of abrasive content upsets or offends me, but one aspect of the show, I learned, energizes my flesh. The sincere *pessimism* of *Black Mirror* tempts me. Part of my particular bent—my flesh—is a kind of nihilistic wallowing in despair. When in pain and avoiding God, I will relish thoughts of abject hopelessness. On more than one occasion, God has asked me to stop doing this. I was surprised one evening to discover that when this behavior was entertained, *Black Mirror* aggravated it. I was already down, melancholy, and *Black Mirror* seemed to confirm my misery. Yeah, I thought, watching it. Everything *is* miserable. I learned that there are times when it's best for me to abstain from *Black Mirror*.

Or how about this one. I find the work of director Lars von Trier fascinating. When he released his two-part epic *Nymphomaniac*, which was without an MPA rating and boasted generous amounts of graphic, unstimulated sex, I knew I would pass on this particular contribution to his already divisive filmography. I suspect that both volumes of *Nymphomaniac* are, in their own ways, excellent works of filmmaking and likely intelligent, challenging, visually arresting. Since I haven't seen it, I don't know how

Nymphomaniac deals with sex, but the press surrounding the film has led me to believe that there are enough extended graphic sequences of actual people having it that I think it in my best interest to sit this one out. On the other hand, another Lars von Trier movie, *The House That Jack Built*, generated perhaps more controversy when it prompted a mass exodus during its screening at the Cannes Film Festival. One article claimed, "A steady stream of patrons fled the theater, many of them looking furious or muttering under their breath. By the time the end credits had stopped rolling, the balcony of the theater was half empty. Nevertheless, the movie still received a prolonged standing ovation for von Trier, who is regarded as a cinematic visionary in France."[2] This movie I did watch. And though it was without sexuality, it was certainly not the kind of movie I'd recommend over tea. Why see this one and not the other?

Because I know that, based on my own bents and brokenness, actual explicit footage of real people having sex could activate lust in me. A stylized cinematic narrative about a serial killer doing horrible things, on the other hand, does not incite me to sin. Of course, "not sinning" is far from the only consideration in choosing what we do and do not observe and enjoy, but I found in *The House That Jack Built* a fascinating meditation on art, suffering, and even evil. The craftsmanship was predictably excellent. The depth of it was readily apparent. Someone else (many other people, I wager) would probably be troubled by scenes in *The House*

That Jack Built to the degree that they'd rather not see them. And that's fine. Each of us must continue in the spiritual discipline of exposing and confronting our flesh so that we can better understand what provokes it. Even an outstanding work of art with many redeeming qualities could energize a particular person's propensity to sin. It falls on that person to exercise discriminating judgment in what they enjoy. There are also ways to navigate discriminating judgment within the context of a single work of art. You might enjoy an album, but skip a song. You might see a movie, but look away for a minute or two. You might read a novel but pass over a few pages. Two people might do this differently. Art that is permissible and good for one person could be damaging and forbidden for another.

To know which is which, we utilize common sense, an analysis of our thinking and feeling, and we ask God, *Is this okay?* It's never enough to simply conclude, Well, I don't *feel* any qualms, so this must be fine. Why? Because you are screwed up. Your "feeling" alone is unreliable. It is only *one* component in navigating right living. And none of this happens in a vacuum. Following Jesus is always and only carried out in the context of community.

COMMUNITY

This book does not have space to build out an exhaustive case for community.[3] Instead, I—like the authors of the New Testament—simply presuppose that the only venue for discipleship to Jesus is community, and that community is the primary context for our spiritual formation. By "community," I mean maintaining intimate, long-term, faithful relationships even across brokenness and interpersonal conflict with a few other disciples of Jesus. I mean knowing one another well. I mean carrying one other's burdens. I mean wrestling through discipleship, with all its messy trial and error, as a family. I mean celebrating and suffering together. And I mean coming together in consistent, disciplined rhythms to study the Scriptures, worship, pray, eat and drink, and take communion. I mean church. Sure, church is a mess (because there are *people* there), but it's the only way to live out discipleship to Jesus. The for-profit enterprise of whining about the church's mistakes is a boring cliché that always assumes the individual knows better. But Jesus and Paul disagree: If you want to do this thing, you have to link arms with screwed-up people. And you're one of them too.

If you think you can follow Jesus all by yourself, without community, without church, you are isolating yourself from what the Bible assumes will be one of our primary sources of growth and the way we access maturity, discernment, and conviction. That is, *other* disciples of Jesus. People who want to follow Jesus without letting other Christians into the process set themselves up to be the ultimate arbiter of their own spirituality, behavior, maturity, and emotional health. Anyone who has maintained relationships with people who love them knows well enough, some of our most significant moments of repentance and growth come on the heels of another Christian faithful enough to hold us accountable for the way we live. That to say, when you exercise discernment, seek God's Spirit, you still need other disciples of Jesus who know and love you to ask, *are you making good decisions* when they lovingly suspect the contrary.

There exists a popular idea that to love someone, you never question or critique their lifestyle or moral judgment. It should go without saying that this idea is incompatible with following Jesus, but let me say it anyway. To follow Jesus, one must operate within community, which means opening oneself to the vulnerability of other people speaking into their lives. Disciples of Jesus presuppose that we are not always accurate assessors of our own lives. We have blind spots. Our perception is faulty. We need faithful brothers and sisters with whom we share our lives to exercise the love and bravery necessary to confront our unhealthiness and sin. To do this, they need relational equity with the people in their community. When they do this well, it will not be noisy, rude, or self-righteous. It will not be brash, condemning, or smug. Instead, it will come as loving and gentle, but also unambiguous and direct. To know whether it's a good time to confront a brother or a sister, ask yourself if any part of you is delighted to do so, if you are eager to expose their folly, if you feel frustration or disgust rather than heartbreak and empathy. If you answer yes to any of those questions, repent and try again. When you do confront another disciple of Jesus about the art they observe and enjoy, only do so with your own theology of art intact—understanding that conviction varies, that art is essential but complicated, that what seems dangerous to you might not be dangerous or sinful for someone else. Many Christians have been confronted by other Christians about their taste in art and entertainment, but I know very few who have been confronted by other Christians who had a healthy theology of art before they did the confronting. So, with your relational equity, empathy, gentleness, humility, and healthy theology of art at the ready, ask that person in your community about art. Finally, and this is important, be prepared to listen to the person you're confronting, to hear them, and to entertain the possibility you could be wrong. And when you're the one being confronted, follow all the same rules.

A Christian's critique of another Christian's choices could be mistaken, and so could the other's defense of those choices. This only works if you're willing to walk with one another, to keep the conversation open, to commit to loving one another with faithfulness to the lordship of Jesus and acceptance of the fact that, sure, people are the worst, but we need people to help us follow Jesus.

EPILOGUE

MY FOUR-YEAR-OLD SON DRAWS AN EXECUTION

ONE MORNING IN 2011, four individuals wearing sunglasses entered a French museum carrying a hammer inside a sock. They had come to destroy a work of art.

But imagine four different disciples of Jesus crowded around Andrew Serrano's controversial *Piss Christ*. The figure of Jesus is still there, still hanging on the cross, still suspended in a jar of urine. The first of the four is offended. For him, the image of Jesus being executed is so sacred, so anchored in the Biblical narrative, that to see this photographed prop—crass and grotesque—is unpleasant. The second person feels less precious about the sacredness of the image itself, nor any visceral offense at the suggestion of pee. On the other hand, they can't help but admire the photograph's composition, lighting, color, and atmosphere. It may be gross conceptually, but it's also kind of lovely in appearance— kind of well done. The third individual doesn't really care about the image or the craftsmanship that birthed it. They don't know much about photography and even less about "fine art." They just sort of shrug. But the fourth person is in tears. Raw as an exposed wound, they stand before *Piss Christ* in repentant brokenness. "It's me," they gasp. "I am the one who has—with my life—profaned the image of Jesus." Breathing deep, aware of their own sin, this fourth person meditates on the incredible kindness of a God who would lovingly give of himself despite so heinous a desecration. Steeped in humanity's filth, and yet laying down his life to save them. The fourth person is compelled to worship.

Turning to one another, each of the four relays their experience of *Piss Christ*. The group affirms the first, who had been offended. Sure, they say, it is, in a certain sense anyway, offensive. There is no requirement for this first person to be unoffended. The group hears from the second, and is encouraged by his eye for technical detail. By this second person's testimony, the group sees something they had missed before and is appreciative. Hearing from the first two, the third person is heartened, and while the piece still fails to stir them, they can acknowledge and celebrate its power to affect others and its viability in doing so. With an open mind, they debate some of the piece's merit with the others.

Finally, each of them acknowledges and celebrates the experience of the fourth person. That the fourth among them was moved, stirred to the conviction of repentance by this offensive image was noteworthy and good—the experience of the piece, though unique among the four, was important. Had any of them imposed their own unique understanding of *Piss Christ* on the other—on anyone else—it would have been disrespectful and devaluing to the others, to the artist, to the art itself—and even to God. If the offended person had censored, vandalized, or demanded the group turn a blind eye to *Piss Christ*, they would have robbed the others of the opportunity to admire, to learn, to worship, and to repent.

And so, the book ends with an appropriately unresolved narrative coda—four disciples of Jesus look at a work of art, each of them drawing from it distinctly different meanings. And that's just fine.

The first time my son drew Jesus, it was the scene of Jesus's death. I keep the picture tucked safely in a drawer so that nothing happens to it. It is one of my favorite works of art. He was four years old when he drew it. Both thieves are represented on Jesus's right and left, but Jesus himself, larger and more detailed, takes center stage. He is represented as a traditional stickman, splayed on a crude-looking cross. With a red crayon, my son depicted blood running in big raindrops down Jesus's face. It looks as if Jesus is crying tears of blood. Jesus's mouth is a pronounced frown. With disproportionate scrawled letters, he inscribed the caption, *Sad Jesus*.

There are many things I love about this drawing, chief among them, of course, being that my son drew it and I love him and that the picture is of Jesus, and I love him as well. But what fascinates me about the image is how stark and upsetting it is to behold. When my son shared the piece with other adults, some of them looked away, others made sad, disapproving sounds, not knowing what to say. One person encouraged him to "draw something happy next time."

My son did not draw this to be cute or garner acclaim (both things he has since learned to do, on occasion, with his art). I know him well enough to know that the image was simply on his mind. He had been filled with questions about Jesus and the cross that Spring, and drawing it was one way to process whatever it was he was feeling, come to grips with it, understand, and deal with it. And the image is heartbreaking. Among our conversations about Jesus and the cross, I don't remember mentioning Jesus's emotional state during his execution. And yet, this is the thing my son chose to highlight in depicting it. *Sad Jesus*. This, to me, encompasses my deep and complicated love for art—that it stirs the heart and the senses. This little drawing, "Sad Jesus," reminds me that art brings us to the deep wells of love and to the bleak valleys of pain like few things can.

And in both places, God is there.

THANK YOU.

THIS BOOK SURVIVED SEVERAL iterations before settling into this particular shape. Professor Todd Miles advocated for it, in premise, as a worthwhile study when I was one of his grad students, and Professor David Nystrom read and graded an early version. Without their encouragement, I doubt it would have survived. My agent, Amanda Luedeke, fought for the book against a depressingly platform-driven publishing industry that values social media followings over actual writing. Arguments in this book first took shape across many good-natured debates with my friend, John Mark Comer, about *Deadpool*. So, thanks to them both. Members of the Order of the Tarrasque—Patrick Porter, Matt Hughes, Gavin Bennett, and Michael Dumont—read early drafts and shared notes. I took them. Rick McKinley has given me a sense of spiritual sanity these last few years. The staff and leadership of Van City Church—including Cameron Silsbee, Levi Warren, Scott Bargaehr, Erik Tabinowski, Katie VanDomelen, Keana Zoradi, Taylor Long, Jan Lampe, Tiffany Erikson, and Lexi Lauser, have been supportive of me and my writing. Beck, Isla, and Arlo have inspired me more than any artist could ever ask. And Abigail has done more than could ever be captured in a 'thank you' section.

NOTES

PREFACE TO ACT I

[1] David Ng, "A Survey of heated rhetoric on Andres Serrano's 'Piss Christ'" *Los Angeles Times*, April 19, 2011, https://www.latimes.com/archives/blogs/culture-monster-blog/story/2011-04-19/a-survey-of-heated-rhetoric-on-andres-serranos-piss-christ

[2] Isaiah 52v14

[3] Vincent Noce, "Andres Serrano: I have No Sympathy For Blasphemy," *Libération,* April 19, 2011, https://next.liberation.fr/arts/2011/04/19/andres-serrano-i-have-no-sympathy-for-blasphemy_730482

[4] "Sister Wendy on Piss Christ (Part 6)," Sister Wendy Beckett, Jun 26, 2007, YouTube video, 1:19, https://youtu.be/L9pAKdkJh-Y

[5] Amanda Holpuch, "Andres Serrano's controversial Piss Christ goes on view in New York," *The Guardian*, September 28, 2012, https://www.theguardian.com/artanddesign/2012/sep/28/andres-serrano-piss-christ-new-york

[6] Lucy Lippard, "Andres Serrano, The Spirit and The Letter," *Art in America,* April, 1990, https://www.artnews.com/art-in-america/features/andres-serrano-provocative-work-lucy-lippard-1234652353/

CHAPTER 1:1

[1] James Dunlevie, "Dark Mofo: Anger, exhilaration in wake of Nitsch 150.Action Hobart performance," *ABC*, June 18, 2017, https://www.abc.net.au/news/2017-06-19/dark-mofo-hermann-nitsch-150action-fallout-goes-on/8629544?utm_campaign=abc_news_web&utm_content=link&utm_medium=content_shared&utm_source=abc_news_web

[2] Ирина Соснина, "Hermann Nitsch: 'Some choose paint, I choose blood'," *Cablook*, September 3, 2016, http://www.cablook.com/inspiration-2/22789/?lang=en

[3] Cynthia Freeland, *But is it art?* (New York: Oxford University Press, 2001) xviii.

[4] Leo Tolstoy, *What is Art?* (New York, Penguin Books, 1995)

[5] Nicholas Wolterstorff, *Art in Action* (Grand Rapids: Wm. B. Eerdmans Publishing Co.,1980)

[6] "The Letter." *Seinfeld,* created by Larry David and Jerry Seinfeld, season three, episode twenty, Castle Rock Entertainment, 1992.

[7] "The Letter." *Seinfeld,* created by Larry David and Jerry Seinfeld, season three, episode twenty, Castle Rock Entertainment, 1992.

[8] Stephen King, *On Writing* (New York, Simon & Schuster, 2000) pp. 198-199.

[9] King, *On Writing*, 2000, pp. 198-199.

[10] Goodman, Nelson, *Languages of Art* (Cambridge, Hackett Publishing Company, 1976) 259.

CHAPTER 1:2

[1] Genesis 1v31

[2] Ploegstra, Jeff, "Creation as Art" (2015). Faculty Work: Comprehensive List. Paper 291. http://digitalcollections.dordt.edu/faculty_work/291

[3] John Sailhammer, *The Meaning of the Pentateuch* (Downers Grove: IVP Academic, 2009)

[4] Genesis 1v26

[5] Genesis 1v27-28

[6] Tim Mackie and Jon Collins, Directors. *Image of God*, YouTube, uploaded by The Bible Project, March 2016. https://youtu.be/YbipxLDtY8c

[7] Exodus 25v8-9

[8] Exodus 28v33

[9] See Exodus 26v1 and 28v3

[10] John Calvin, *Commentary on the Psalms* (Grand Rapids: Eerdmans, 1949), commentary on Psalm 9:11, italics added.

[11] Tim Mackie and Jon Collins, Directors. *The Art of Biblical Poetry*, YouTube, uploaded by The Bible Project, May 2018. https://youtu.be/q9yp1ZXbsEg

CHAPTER 1:3

[1] Ezekiel 1v28

[2] 1 Chronicles 23v5

[3] vv20-24

[4] John 6v53

[5] vv52-60

[35] 2 Tim. 3v15-18, 2 Peter 1v21

[36] Exodus 31v18

[6] v61

[7] v67

[8] Matthew 5v28-30

[9] Matthew 13v10

[10] Matthew 13v44-46

[11] Luke 15v11-32

[12] Matthew 24v45-51

[13] Jer 8v11-13, Hosea 9v10, Micah 7v1-2

[14] Exodus 31v18

[15] C.S. Lewis, *An Experiment in Criticism* (Cambridge: Cambridge University Press, 1961) 141.

[16] Matthew Henry, *Matthew Henry's Commentary on the Whole Bible, Song of Solomon*

[17] Matthew 5v43-48, Romans 12v14-21, 1 Peter 3v8

2 Chron 3v6

[18] Ezekiel 17v1-2

[19] Stephen King, *On Writing,* (New York, Simon & Schuster, 2000) 190.

CHAPTER 2:1

[1] Ira Silverberg, *Word Virus* (New York: Grove Press, 1998) xiii

[2] Oz, Frank (TheFrankOzJam). "Sesame Street. Early '70's. We're rehearsing a "Rapunzel" sketch. Jon Stone directing. We're screwing around. Tears in our eyes from laughing. I shout to Jon, "What are we teaching?" Jon shouts back,"Who cares!" And he was right. Sometimes just having fun has value all it's own." 3 Feb 2018, 11:02 PM. Tweet.

[3] Francis Schaeffer, *Art and the Bible,* (Downers Grove: Inter-Varisty Press, 1973) 50.

[4] Schaeffer, *Art and the Bible,* 1973, 26.

[5] Schaeffer, *Art and the Bible,* 1973, 27.

CHAPTER 2:2

[1] Arthur Danto, *The Artworld,* The Journal of Philosophy, Vol. 61, No. 19, American Philosophical Association Eastern Division Sixty-First Annual Meeting. (Oct. 15, 1964), pp. 571-584.

[2] Eric Ditzian, "Black Swan' Director Darren Aronofsky on Ballet, Natalie Portman and Lesbian Kisses*" MTV*, Viacom International Inc., 30 August 2010, http://www.mtv.com/news/1646763/black-swandirector-darren-aronofsky-on-ballet-natalie-portman-and-lesbian-kisses/.

[3] Philip Graham Ryken, *Art for God's Sake* (Phillipsburg: P&R Publishing, 2006) 13.

[4] Martin Scorsese, "Martin Scorsese: I Said Marvel Movies Aren't Cinema. Let Me Explain." *The New York Times*, November, 4

2019, https://www.nytimes.com/2019/11/04/opinion/martin-scorsese-marvel.html

5 Andrew Blair, "19 Ambitious Movies That Didn't Go as Planned," *Den of Geek,* January 30, 2017, https://www.denofgeek.com/movies/19-ambitious-movies-that-didnt-go-as-planned/

6 Gabriella Paiella, "Nicolas Cage Can Explain It All" *GQ,* March 22, 2022 https://www.gq.com/story/nicolas-cage-april-cover-profile

CHAPTER 3:1

1 *Dogma.* Lion's Gate, 1999.

2 Belinda Cleary, "Furious parents switch off 'gross and fatphobic' Bluey episode - but others defend the show: 'It's about health'" *The Daily Mail,* April 16, 2023 https://www.dailymail.co.uk/femail/article-11979557/Bluey-exercise-episode-slammed-fatphobic-mums-said-important-avoid-obesity.html

58 Steve Rabey, "Religion Journal; A Chastened Singer Returns to Christian Basics" *The New York Times,* May 11, 2002, https://www.nytimes.com/2002/05/11/us/religion-journala-chastened-singer-returns-to-christian-basics.html

3 Jerram Barr, *Echoes of Eden* (Wheaton: Crossway, 2013) 18.

4 John Calvin, *On the Life of the Christian Man* (Grand Rapids: Baker, 1952), 88.

5 Jerram Barr, *Echoes of Eden* (Wheaton: Crossway, 2013) 11, 31.

6 John Mark Comer, *Garden City* (Grand Rapids: Zondervan,

2015) 98.

[7] Philip Graham Ryken, *Art for God's Sake* (Phillipsburg: P&R Publishing, 2006) 34.

[8] C.S. Lewis, "Christianity and Literature," *Genesis: Journal of the Society of Christians in the Arts, Inc.* 1, no. 2 (1974) 14.

[9] Bishop Robert Barron. *On Art and the Glory of God*, YouTube, uploaded by Bishop Robert Barron, August 2018. https://youtu.be/BLuGvBSinn4

[10] Frank Scheck, "'Unplanned': Film Review," *The Hollywood Reporter*, March 29, 2019, https://www.hollywoodreporter.com/review/unplanned-1198201

[11] Thomas Merton, *The Sign of Jonas* (New York, Harcourt Inc, 2002) 59-60.

[12] Exodus 31v2-4

[13] Ex. 26v1, 28:3, 31v1-6

[14] Stanley Hauerwas, *Matthew* (Grand Rapids, Bazos Press, 2009) 127.

[15] Matthew 13v11-13

[16] Isaiah 6v8-13

[17] France, R.T. *The Gospel of Matthew* (Grand Rapids, Eerdmans Publishing Co., 2007) 502.

[18] 2 Samuel 13v15

CHAPTER 3:2

[19] Roger Cohen, "Bret Easton Ellis Answers Critics of 'American Psycho'" *The New York Times*, March 6, 1991,

https://www.nytimes.com/1991/03/06/books/bret-easton-el-lisanswers-critics-of-american-psycho.html

[20] S.M. Sterling, *The Conquistador*, (New York City, Ace, 2004)

[21] Trey Taylor, "How American Psycho Became a Feminist Statement" *Dazed*, August 19, 2014, http://www.dazeddigital.com/artsandculture/article/20751/1/how-american-psycho-became-a-feministstatement

[22] *Ricky Gervais: Humanity*, directed by John L. Spencer (Netflix Studios, 2018)

[23] For more on the controversial, clandestine nature of the American trade association that assigns movies their ratings, see the 2006 documentary *This Film Is Not Yet Rated*.

[24] John 19v1

[25] Mark 14v65

[26] Matthew 27v26

[27] Ebert, Roger "The Passion of the Christ," *RogerEbert.Com*, February 24, 2004, https://www.rogerebert.com/reviews/the-passion-of-the-christ-2004.

[28] David Edelstein, "Jesus H. Christ" *Slate*, February 24, 2004, https://slate.com/culture/2004/02/the-passion-mel-gibson-s-bloody-mess.html

[29] Tom Neven, "The Passion of the Christ" *Plugged In*, https://www.pluggedin.com/movie-reviews/passionofthechrist/

[30] Neven, Tom "Exorcist: The Beginning" *Plugged In,* Focus on the Family, https://www.pluggedin.com/movie-reviews/exorcistthebeginning/

[31] *Ratatouille*, directed by Brad Bird, (Pixar Animation Studios, 2007).

[32] Ezekiel 37v8

[33] Thought I appreciate Calvin's defense of art, I disagree with him profoundly on the major points of his namesake theological system.

[34] John Calvin, *Institutes of the Christian Religion*, trans. Henry Beveridge, rev. ed. (Peabody, MA: Hendrickson, 2008), 2.2.15.

CHAPTER 3:3

[1] Eric Weisbard, "Trent Reznor: Sympathy for the Devil" *Spin*, February, 1996

[2] David Kerr, "Came Back Vaunted: An Interview with Nine Inch Nails' Trent Reznor" *The Skinny*, May 6, 2014, https://www.theskinny.co.uk/music/interviews/came-back-vaunted-an-interview-with-nine-inch-nails-trent-reznor

[3] ExtraDistressrial. "What is everyone's issue with Big Man With a Gun?." Reddit. Accessed November 7, 2023. https://www.reddit.com/r/nin/comments/wkq3i8/what_is_everyones_issue_with_big_man_with_a_gun/.

[4] Ottessa Moshfegh, "The dark brilliance of Bret Easton Ellis" *The Guardian*, March 2, 2019, https://www.theguardian.com/books/2019/mar/02/evil-under-the-sun-the-darkbrilliance-of-bret-easton-ellis

[5] See "The Student, the Fish, and Professor Agassiz," *American*

Poems (3rd ed,; Boston: Houghton, Osgood and Co., 1879) pp. 450-54

[6] *Best Worst Movie,* Directed by Michael P. Stephenson, (Magicstone Productions, New Video Group, 2009)

[7] Ruiz, Michelle "Why I Won't Be Seeing the New *Joker* Movie" *Vogue*, October 7, 2019, https://www.vogue.com/article/joker-movie-controversy

[8] Peter Travers and Joaquin Phoenix. *Joaquin Phoenix on the making of 'Joker'*, YouTube, uploaded by Popcorn with Peter Travers, October, 2019 https://youtu.be/7WqVB7OcERU

[9] "The Customer's Usually Right," *Wings*, created by David Angell, Peter Case, and David Lee, season four, episode ten, Grub Street Productions, Paramount Network Television, 1992.

[10] Ephesians 2v3

[11] Romans 7v5

[12] 2 Peter 2v10

[13] 1 Corinthians 7v1-7

[14] Peter Helman, "Nick Cave Addresses Whether He'll Change Problematic Old Lyrics" *Stereogum*, March 7, 2020, https://www.stereogum.com/2076046/nick-cave-addresses-changeproblematic-old-lyrics/news/

[15] Ariana Lange, "Drawing the Line, The Disturbing Secret Behind An Iconic Cartoon: Underage Sexual Abuse" *BuzzFeed News*, March 29, 2018, https://www.buzzfeednews.com/article/ariane-lange/john-kricfalusi-ren-stimpy-underage-sexual-abuse

[16] Atkinson, R. (2012, February 10). Reform Section 5 speech

[Speech transcript]. Retrieved from http://reformsection5.org.uk/2012/10/rowan-atkinsons-speech-at-rs5-parliamentary-reception/

[17] Jerry Mitchell, "Here's the proof against Carolyn Bryant Donham in the Emmett Till case. Is it enough to convict her?" *The Boston Globe*, July 14, 2022, https://www.bostonglobe.com/2022/07/14/opinion/heres-proof-against-carolyn-bryant-donham-emmett-till-case-is-it-enough-convict-her/

[18] Alex Greenberger, "'The Painting Must Go': Hannah Black Pens Open Letter to the Whitney About Controversial Biennial Work" *ARTnews*, March 21, 2017 https://www.artnews.com/artnews/news/the-painting-must-go-hannah-black-pens-open-letter-to-the-whitney-about-controversial-biennial-work-7992/

[19] Dayna Evans, "In an Open Letter, Artists Are Asking the Whitney to Take Down a Painting of Emmett Till" *The Cut*, March 21 2017, https://www.thecut.com/2017/03/whitney-biennialemmett-till-dana-schutz.html

[20] Basciano Oliver, "Whitney Biennial: Emmett Till casket painting by white artist sparks anger." *The Guardian*, March 27, 2017, https://www.theguardian.com/artanddesign/2017/mar/21/whitney-biennial-emmett-till-painting-danaschutz

[21] Fusco Coco, "Censorship, Not the Painting, Must Go: On Dana Schutz's Image of Emmett Till" *Hyperallergic*, March 27, 2017, https://hyperallergic.com/368290/censorship-notthe-painting-

must-go-on-dana-schutzs-image-of-emmett-till/

[22] *Ricky Gervais: Humanity*, directed by John L. Spencer (Netflix Studios, 2018)

[23] Ron Charles, "Oprah refused to cancel her 'American Dirt' show — and reminded us what civil discourse looks like" *The Washington Post*, March 6, 2020, https://www.washingtonpost.com/entertainment/books/oprah-refused-to-cancel-her-american-dirt-show-and-reminded-us-what-civil-discourse-looks-like/2020/03/06/032a9404-5fbc-11ea-b014-4fafa866bb81_story.html

[24] Billboard Staff, "Spotify Removes Hate Music as Streaming Companies Struggle to Police Their Tunes" *Billboard*, August 16, 2017, https://www.billboard.com/pro/spotify-removes-hate-band-music-streaming/

[25] Dan Rys, "Spotify Removes R. Kelly Music From Its Playlists As Part of New Hate Content & Hateful Conduct Policy: Exclusive" *Billboard*, Billboard, May 10, 2018,
https://www.billboard.com/articles/business/8455375/spotify-removes-r-kelly-music-playlists-new-hatecontent-conduct-policy

[26] Carlos Aguilar, "'The Secret Life of Pets 2' Film Review: Cartoon Offers Outdated Messages About Marriage, Manliness" *The Wrap*, May 23, 2019, https://www.thewrap.com/the-secret-life-of-pets-2-film-review-patton-oswalt-harrison-ford/

CHAPTER 3:4

[1] Chris Evangelista, "'Dragged Across Concrete' Review: A Nasty, Nihilistic Nightmare Designed to Provoke," */Film*, March 21, 2019, https://www.slashfilm.com/dragged-across-concrete-review/

[2] Chris Evangelista, "'Dragged Across Concrete' Review," */Film*

[3] Roger Ebert, *The Great Movies*, (New York: Crown/Archetype, 2008) 62.

[4] Jerry Seinfeld (2017) "Jerry Seinfeld Talks Bill Cosby, Whether He Can Separate The Man From The Body Of Art" Interview with Stephen Colbert. *The Late Show with Stephen Colbert*. CBS. September 30, 2017

[5] Jerry Seinfeld, Interview with Stephen Colbert, September 30, 2017

[6] Jerry Seinfeld, Interview with Stephen Colbert, September 30, 2017

[7] Samuel 13v14, Acts 13v22

[8] See Alexander Abasili's *Was It Rape?: The David and Bathsheba Pericope Re-Examined*, and Denny Burk's *Adultery or Rape? What happened between David and Bathsheba?*

[9] Psalm 51

[10] Smith, Russell "Good art by bad people: Why it shouldn't be thrown away," *The Globe and Mail*, November 16, 2017, https://www.theglobeandmail.com/arts/good-art-by-bad-peoplewhy-it-shouldnt-be-thrown-away/article37006883/

[11] Russell Smith, "Good art by bad people: Why it shouldn't be

thrown away," *The Globe and Mail*, November 16, 2017, https://www.theglobeandmail.com/arts/good-art-by-bad-peoplewhy-it-shouldnt-be-thrown-away/article37006883/

[12] James Poniewozik, "Bad Deeds Don't Ruin Great Art," *Time* , January 13, 2014, https://time.com/682/bad-deeds-dont-ruin-great-art/

[13] For more on the imact of *The Ren & Stimpy Show* and the accusations lobbied at John Kricfalusi, see the fascinating documentary film, *Happy Happy Joy Hoy: The Ren & Stimpy Story*

[14] Joe Flint, "'Simpsons' Episode Featuring Michael Jackson's Voice to Be Pulled," *The Wall Street Journal,* March 19, 2019, https://www.wsj.com/articles/simpsons-episodefeaturing-michael-jacksons-voice-to-be-pulled-11552007802

[15] Reed, D., Robson, W., & Safechuck, J. (2019). *Leaving Neverland* . HBO Home Entertainment.

[16] Charles McGrath, "Good Art, Bad People," *The New York Times*, June 21, 2012, https://www.nytimes.com/2012/06/22/opinion/global-agenda-magazine-good-art-bad-people.html

[17] Elaine Showalter, "Household Words: The Complicated Domestic Life of Charles Dickens." *The New Republic*, December 6, 2012, https://newrepublic.com/article/110742/household-words

CHAPTER 3:5

[1] Hans R. Rookmaaker, *Art Needs No Justification* (Leicester,

Inter-Varsity Press, 1978) 9.

[2] Philip Graham Ryken, *Art and the Church* (Phillipsburg: P&R Publishing, 2006) 9

[3] *The Rules of Real Life Don't Apply to Art - Rob Zombie*, YouTube, uploaded by JRE Clips, Sep 16 2016. https://youtu.be/Dc4qIH9PndU

[4] Andy Crouch, *For the Beauty of the Church: Casting a Vision for the Arts* (Grand Rapids, Baker Books, 2010) 41.

[5] Marty Beckerman, "Bret Easton Ellis, Imperial Bedrooms, Interview" *Daily Beast*, July 14, 2017 https://www.thedailybeast.com/bret-easton-ellis-imperial-bed-rooms-inter-view#:~:text=%E2%80%9CI%20don't%20think%20about,cash%20and%20too%20little%20compassion.

[6] Brad Wieners, "Color Him a Provocateur" *Wired*, December 1, 1996, https://www.wired.com/1996/12/kalman/

[7] Tom Breihan, "Nick Cave Says Kanye Is Our Greatest Artist Right now," *Stereogum*, Stereogum Media, LLC, January 17, 2020, https://www.stereogum.com/2070368/nick-cave-says-kanye-is-our-greatest-artistright-now/news/

[8] Stanley Hauerwas, *Matthew* (Grand Rapids: Brazos Pres, 2006) 128.

[9] Matthew 10v22

[10] A.W. Tozer, *The Crucified Life* (Grand Rapids: Baker, 2011) 124.

[11] Thomas Merton, *New Seeds of Contemplation* (Cambridge: New Directions, 1961) 44.

[12] Galatians 5v12

CHAPTER 4:1

[1] Blackmore, Jex "A Letter From Jex Blackmore" Feb 01, 2016, http://satanicrevolution.com/index.html#two

[2] Job 17v14, KJV

[3] Blackmore, Jex "A Letter From Jex Blackmore" Feb 01, 2016, http://satanicrevolution.com/index.html#two

[4] Eugene H. Peterson, *The Pastor: A Memoir* (San Francisco: HarperOne, 2001) 164.

[5] Peterson, *The Pastor: A Memoir*, 2001, 164.

[6] Peterson, *The Pastor: A Memoir*, 2001, 164.

[7] IndieWire Filmmaker Toolkit, "The Witch Director Robert Eggers," https://soundcloud.com/user-445966404/the-witch-director-robert-eggers

CHAPTER 4:2

[1] Dan Kedmey, "How the Sistine Chapel spawned a public relations nightmare" *Ideas.Ted.Com,* Jan 26, 2016, https://ideas.ted.com/how-the-sistine-chapel-spawned-a-public-relationsnightmare/

[2] Elizabeth Lev, "The Unheard Story of the Sistine Chapel," ted.com, December 2015, https://www.ted.com/talks/elizabeth_lev_the_unheard_story_of_the_sistine_chapel?language=en

³ John Piper, "God Has a People for His Name" *Desiring God*, June 25, 2016, https://wwww.desiringgod.org/articles/god-has-a-people-for-his-name

⁴ Song of Solomon 4v5-6

⁵ Song of Solomon 2v3

⁶ Stieg Larsson, *The Girl with the Dragon Tattoo*, (New York, Vintage Crime/Black Lizard, 2011) 11

⁷ Ingrid Solano, Nicholas R. Eaton, Daniel O'Leary, "Pornography Consumption, Modality and Function in a Large Internet Sample," *Journal of sex research*, October 25, 2018, https://doi.org/10.1080/00224499.2018.1532488

⁸ Irvine Welsh, "American Psycho is a modern classic," *The Guardian*, January 10, 2015 https://www.theguardian.com/books/2015/jan/10/american-psycho-bret-eastonellis-irvine-welsh

CHAPTER 4:3

⁹ Katherine Dunn, *One Cussing: Bad Words and Creative Cursing* (New York, Tin House Books, 2019) pp. 31-32.

¹⁰ Stephen King, *On Writing,* (New York, Simon & Schuster, 2000) pp.184-185.

¹¹ Katherine Dunn, *One Cussing: Bad Words and Creative Cursing* (New York, Tin House Books, 2019) 18.

CHAPTER 4:4

¹ "Janet Maslin, FILM REVIEW; Panoramic and Personal Visions

of War's Anguish," *The New York* Times, July 24, 1998 https://www.nytimes.com/1998/07/24/movies/film-review-pano-ramic-and-personal-visions-of-war-s-anguish.html

2 Brian De Palma, "Brian De Palma on *Snake Eyes*," Interview by Henri Béhar, *Film Scouts*, http://www.film-scouts.com/scripts/interview.cfm?File=bri-dep

3 Mark D. Griffiths, Ph.D, "Why Do We Like Watching Scary Films? A brief look at psychological horror at the cinema" *Psychology Today*, Sussex Publishers, LLC , October 29, 2015 https://www.psychologytoday.com/us/blog/in-excess/201510/why-do-we-watching-scary-films

4 I recommend Preston Sprinkle's excellent book, *Fight: A Christian Case for Nonviolence*

5 Philip Graham Ryken, *Art for God's Sake*, (Phillipsburg: P&R Publishing, 2006) 13.

CODA 1

1 See Pete Greig's excellent *How to Hear God: A Simple Guide for Normal People*.

2 Ramin Setoodeh, "Lars von Trier's 'The House That Jack Built' Causes Walkouts and Outrage at Cannes," *Variety*, May 14, 2018, https://variety.com/2018/film/news/lars-von-triersthe-house-that-jack-built-causes-walkouts-and-outrage-at-cannes-1202810582/

3 Joseph H. Hellerman's *When the Church Was a Family,* Richard Plass and James Cofield's *The Relational Soul*, and Dietrich Bonhoeffer's *Life Together* are some books that do.

ABOUT THE AUTHOR

Joshua S. Porter is pastor of teaching and creative vision at Van City Church in Vancouver, Washington. He is also a former member of the experimental art-punk band, Showbread, and the author of the *Death to Deconstruction* and the novel *Punk Rock Vs. the Lizard People.*

Find out more and connect with Joshua at **joshuasporter.com**.

www.ingramcontent.com/pod-product-compliance
Lightning Source LLC
Chambersburg PA
CBHW020336180726
47991CB00020B/1715